PATTERNS
for Making
AMISH DOLLS
and Doll Clothes

PATTERNS
for Making
AMISH DOLLS
and Doll Clothes

Rachel Pellman and Jan Steffy

Good Books

Intercourse, Pennsylvania 17534

Design by Craig N. Heisey
Cover photo by Jonathan Charles
Inside photos by Kenneth Pellman

Patterns for Making Amish Dolls and Doll Clothes
© 1987 by Good Books, Intercourse, PA 17534
International Standard Book Number: 0-934672-47-4
Library of Congress Catalog Card Number: 87-23700

Library of Congress Cataloging-in-Publication Data
Pellman, Rachel T. (Rachel Thomas)
    Patterns for making Amish dolls and doll clothes.

    Bibliography: p.
    1. Dollmaking. 2. Doll clothes. I. Steffy, Jan,
1967–. II. Title. III. Title: Amish dolls and doll clothes.
TT175.P45   1987   745.592′21   87-23700
ISBN 0-934672-47-4

Table of Contents

Introduction

To an outsider, the Amish way of life can appear restricted and inhibiting. Certainly, the Amish community creates clear boundaries within which its members function. These boundaries, however, provide a sense of identity and belonging that many people in the modern world lack.

Amish folk art gives witness to the freedom that can be found within the confines of the community. Amish quilts, especially those of the early 20th century, combine visual appeal with quality workmanship. Their uninhibited use of color, along with a careful construction born of practicality, has made them widely sought by quilt lovers and collectors.

Dolls and Values

In a similar way, Amish dolls show the values of Amish life. Old dolls (before 1940) and the dolls found among the more conservative groups today are homemade out of cloth. Their most distinctive charac-teristic is their lack of facial features. This is in keeping with the Old Testament commandment against making graven images. Facial features were considered to be too much in the likeness of a human being and were therefore discouraged.

At the same time, the variety of Amish dolls belies the myth that everyone in the Amish community dresses, thinks and acts alike. The Amish indeed believe that faith can best be lived within the context of a community, and maintain common practices that separate them from the outside world. Most Old Order groups use horses and carriages for transportation, dress in a modest and distinctive style, do not use electricity in their houses and speak a German dialect (Pennsylvania German, erroneously called "Dutch") at home. Nevertheless, there are many communities of Amish, each with slightly differing practices. As with any group, there are also individual differences of personality and taste.

It is not surprising, then, that Amish dolls vary widely in form and degree of finish. Some dolls have a crude style and proportions. Others are carefully designed and clothed in detailed layers mirroring the Amish way of dress. Some dolls have contours which provide a sense of facial lines without the addition of eyes, nose and mouth. Others have flat, lollipop-style heads.

Lizzie Lapp Dolls

Though many dolls were made by mothers, aunts or grandmothers and given to children, individuals within the Amish community occasionally made a specialty of doll-making, developing a distinctive style. One such doll-maker was Lizzie Lapp, who lived in Lancaster County, Pennsylvania, from 1860 to 1932. Although she suffered from a severe speech impediment, she was adept with her hands. The dolls she made and sold from her home were constructed in three basic units. The head, trunk and arms were one section. The legs and feet—the second section—were attached separately so that the doll could sit. The final section was the hands, which were attached to the arms in a glove-like fashion.

The hands of Lizzie's dolls were made of denim. They were constructed similarly to a mitten, with a moveable thumb, but the hand was stitched to provide the outline of the remaining four fingers. The feet, also made of denim, extended partway up the leg like a boot. The head of each doll was covered with a sheath which was white on one side and black on the other. The sheath was handstitched at the shoulder and gave the effect of hair on one side of the head and face on the other.

Lizzie buried a stick in the stuffing of her dolls extending from the doll trunk through the neck and into the head. This kept the head from becoming floppy after hours of loving play. Lizzie's dolls wore a simple Amish dress but no covering or bonnet.

Amish Dolls Today

Today, many Amish dolls are store-bought. But the large majority of them are clothed with homemade material which mimics the style and color of the owner's clothes. Most Amish clothing is made at home, and leftover scraps can easily be used by a child to make doll clothes. Because most Amish wear only solid colored fabrics, dolls do also. The colors used tend to represent only half of the color wheel, from red-violet to, and including, green. Shirts and dresses in these hues are rich and vibrant when coupled with black pants and vests or capes and aprons. While adults tend to wear the darker, more subdued blues, greens, violets and burgundies, children often wear the bouncier versions of these colors.

There are three basic patterns in this book: a jointed doll based on a 1930 model, in 20- and 12-inch sizes; a Lizzie Lapp doll; and a mini folk-doll. The jointed doll comes with patterns for complete male and female clothing for both children and adults, in the style of the clothes worn by the Amish of Lancaster County, Pennsylvania. The Lizzie Lapp doll dress pattern is a copy of the dress Lizzie's dolls wore. The mini folk-doll comes with patterns for male and female clothes in one size.

Glossary of Terms

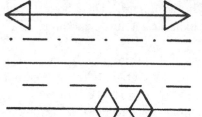

Straight Grain—Place on fabric an even distance from selvage.

Fold—Place on fold of fabric.

Seam Allowance—The area between seam line and cutting line, ¼″ unless otherwise indicated.

Notches—For matching pattern pieces.

Edgestitching—On outside, stitch close to seam or finished edge.

Press—Press seams open unless otherwise stated.

Machine Baste—Machine stitch in largest size stitches to hold together.

Topstitching—On outside, stitch to decorate with medium large straight stitches.

Gather—Machine baste ⅜ inch from raw edge and pull bobbin threads, adjusting fabric to instructed length. Remove gathering threads after sewing seam and securing gathers.

Understitch—Stitch through facing and seam allowances close to seam.

Clean-finish—Sew raw edge with a zig-zag stitch or turn under ¼ inch and edge-stitch.

Interface—Follow manufacturer's instructions for applying interfacing.

Slipstitch—Handstitch, catching a tiny section of fabric so that stitching is invisible.

Staystitch—Machine stitch ¼ inch from raw edge to prevent stretching.

Instructions

Note: The directions for 20- and 12-inch dolls are identical, except as specifically noted. The same number of pieces is used for both sizes. Yardage and fabric color requirements are listed on pg. 19.

Doll

Large Size (4 pieces; patterns on pages 21–29)
Small Size (patterns on pages 151–53)

Doll Body

1. Staystitch entire perimeters of doll-body sides (A) and center (B) sections. Clip edges.
2. With right sides together, pin one doll-body side section to doll-body center section, starting at triple notch and working toward double notch. Continue pinning doll side to doll center section, stopping at square dot at lower edge of side and center sections. Stitch, using a very small, tight stitch, and ease in fullness at curves. Starting again at triple notch, pin side section to center section, stopping at square dot.
3. With right sides together, pin bottom edges of doll-center section together. Stitch from square dot to square dot.
4. With right sides together, pin remaining doll-side section to doll center. Begin at triple notch and stitch down front side of doll to square dot, leaving opening along dotted line for stuffing. Return to triple notch and stitch down back side of doll.
5. Turn doll rightside out. Stuff firmly. Slipstitch opening on doll front.

Doll Arms

1. With right sides together, stitch two arm (C) sections together leaving open along dotted line for stuffing. Clip curves.
2. Turn arms rightside out. Stuff firmly. Slipstitch opening.

Doll Legs

1. With right sides together, stitch two leg (D) sections together leaving open along dotted line for stuffing. Clip curves.
2. Turn legs rightside out. Stuff firmly. Slipstitch opening.

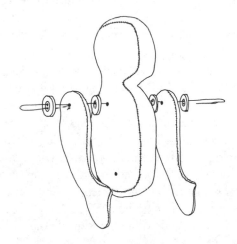

Attaching arms and legs to body

1. Use a very large dollmaking needle, a long double strand of carpet thread and flat, 1-inch buttons (½ inch for 12-inch doll), each with two holes. On outside of arm, make a small stitch approximately ¼ inch away from button dot to secure

9

thread. Insert needle slightly into arm and bring it back out in center of dot. Thread button onto needle.

Reinsert needle through second hole of button, through arm, having needle reemerge at dot on inside of arm. Thread another button onto needle through one hole of button. Go through doll body, entering at dot on one side and emerging at dot on other side of body. Thread needle through a third button through only one hole. Go through second arm inserting needle at dot and emerging at dot. Add a fourth button going through one hole of button and reentering arm through second hole of button. Allow enough slack in thread so arms can be pulled away from body to see where needle is reinserted. Rethread through arms and body, making sure needle enters body and emerges from body at same spot as previously.

Always go through same hole of button on inside of arms. This allows for arms to move freely. Go back through arms and body a third time. Pull thread through tightly, keeping arms snugly secured against body. Wrap thread several times around back of button. Catch fabric to make a secure knot.

2. Repeat for leg attachment.

Adult's Dress

For Large Doll (7 pieces; patterns on pages 31–39)
For Small Doll (patterns on pages 155–57)

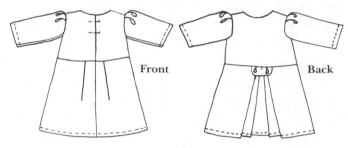

Front   Back

1. Staystitch neck edge and armholes on bodice front and back.

2. With right sides together, stitch bodice front (A) to bodice back (B) at shoulder seams. Press seams open.

3. Turn under ¼ inch on bottom of each sleeve (D). Fold under another ¼ inch and stitch, forming hem for sleeve edge.

4. On sleeve, bring solid lines to dotted lines on either side of center dot to form two small pleats on either side of center. Pleats should fold away from center dot. Baste. With right sides together, pin sleeves to bodice armholes having center dots at shoulder seams and notches matching. Clip where necessary to ease sleeves into position. Stitch. Stitch again ⅛ inch from previous stitching within the seam allowance. Clip curves. Trim seams.

5. With right sides together, pin bodice front and back together at side seams and underarm sleeve seams. Stitch in one continuous seam, matching underarm seams and notches, and keeping sleeve edges even.

6. Staystitch neck edge of neck facing (C). Clean-finish long unnotched edge of facing. With right sides together, pin neck

facing to neck edge, clipping where necessary. Stitch. Clip curves and trim seam. Open facing. Press seam allowance toward facing. Understitch. Clean-finish edge of bodice fronts and facings. Turn facing to inside and press. Tack in place at shoulder seams.

7. Clean-finish extensions of skirt front (E). Make darts in skirt front. Press toward center. With right sides together, pin skirt fronts together. Stitch across bottom of extension, pivoting at corner, and continue stitching down skirt front. Clip seam allowance diagonally at corner of extension so seam can be opened and pressed.

8. With right sides together, stitch leppli pieces (G) together leaving straight edge along top open. Clip curves and trim seam. Turn and press. Match dots and leppli to form a small pleat. (Opening of pleat will be exposed side of leppli.) Baste along upper edge.

9. Fold pleats in skirt back (F), bringing solid lines to meet dotted lines and dotted lines to meet center dot. Pleats should face center of both sides of center back. Baste across top. Center leppli over pleats on skirt back with raw edges even, and then baste in place.

10. With right sides together, stitch skirt front to skirt back at side seams.

11. With right sides together, stitch bodice to skirt, matching side seams and notches.

12. Fold extension to inside along fold lines on right side of bodice and skirt front. Tack in place at neck edge and waist.

Since adult Amish women use straight pins as closures, no buttons or buttonholes are required.

Child's Dress

For Large Doll (6 pieces; patterns on pages 41–49)
For Small Doll (patterns on pages 159–63)

Front   Back

1. Staystitch neck edge and arm holes on bodice front and back.

2. With right sides together, stitch bodice front (A) to bodice backs (B) at shoulder seams. Press seams open.

3. Turn under ¼ inch on bottom edge of each sleeve (C). Fold under another ¼ inch and stitch, forming hem for sleeve edge.

4. On sleeve, bring solid lines to dotted lines on either side of center dot to form two small pleats on each side of center. Pleats should fold away from center dot. Baste. With right sides together, pin each sleeve to respective bodice armhole, keeping center dot at shoulder seam and notches matching. Clip where necessary to ease sleeve into position. Stitch. Stitch again ⅛ inch from previous stitching in seam allowance. Clip curves. Trim seam.

5. With right sides together, pin bodice sides and sleeve seams together. Stitch in one continuous line, matching underarm seams and notches, and keeping sleeve edges even.

6. Staystitch neck edge of neck facing (D). Clean-finish long, unnotched edge of facing. With right sides together, pin neck facing to neck edge, clipping where necessary. Stitch. Clip curves and trim seam. Open facing. Press seam allowance toward facing. Understitch. Clean-finish edges of bodice backs and facings. Turn facing to inside. Tack at shoulder seams and back edges.

7. Clean-finish extensions of skirt back (E). With right sides together, pin backs together. Stitch across bottom of extension and down skirt back. Pivot at corner of extension. Clip to corner of extension. Press seam open. Fold extension along fold line.

8. With right sides together, stitch skirt back to skirt front (F) at sides. Press seams open.

9. Gather along upper edge of skirt front and back. Pin skirt to bodice, matching notches and finished edges of back. Stitch.

10. Turn under ¼ inch on bottom edge of skirt. Fold under and stitch in place to form hem.

11. Make button holes on right side of back. Attach buttons.

Adult's Apron

For Large Doll (2 pieces; patterns on pages 51–53)
For Small Doll (patterns on pages 165)

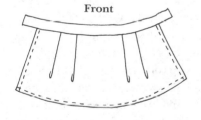

1. Turn under ¼ inch on both sides of apron (A). Turn under another ¼ inch and stitch to hem sides of apron.

2. Turn under ¼ inch of apron hem. Turn under another ¼ inch and stitch to form apron hem.

3. Sew darts in apron front. Press darts toward center.

4. Fold under ¼ inch on long, unnotched edge of apron belt (B) and press.

5. With right sides together, pin belt to apron, matching notches. Belt will extend beyond apron on both sides. Stitch. Trim seam. Press seam toward belt.

6. With right sides together, fold belt portion in half, extending beyond apron. Stitch ends and lower edge of belt to meet previously stitched apron and belt seam. Trim seams. Turn belt extensions rightside out. Bring pressed edge of belt over seam allowance on wrong side of apron. Slipstitch in place.

7. Adult Amish women close their aprons with straight pins. The lower edge of the apron belt should be even with the

waistline of the dress and should cover cape points in front and back. Leppli at the back of the dress should be fully visible underneath the apron belt. Secure apron with straight pins.

Adult's Cape

For Large Doll (2 pieces; patterns on page 55)
For Small Doll (patterns on page 167)

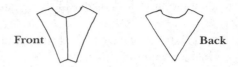

1. Staystitch neck edge. Clean-finish unnotched edge of neck facing (B).

2. With right sides together, pin facing to neck edge of cape (A). Stitch. Clip curves and trim seam. Press seam toward facing. Understitch. Turn facing to inside. Press.

3. Turn under ¼ inch on front opening edges of cape. Turn under another ¼ inch. Trim facing to avoid excess bulk when folded under at neck edge. Slipstitch in place. Slipstitch sides of back in the same way, maintaining a sharp point at lower edge of cape back. Fold under and slipstitch lower edges of cape front.

4. Cape closures are straight pins. The cape should be pinned together at center front. Its lower edges are covered and held in place by the apron belt.

Child's Apron

For Large Doll (4 pieces; patterns on pages 57–63)
For Small Doll (patterns on page 169)

1. Fold apron (A) in half. With wrong sides together, stitch along pleat line from top to large dot. Open apron front and press pleat to form a flat pleat centered under stitching line. On right side of fabric, stitch across pleat horizontally at small dots through all thicknesses.

2. With right sides together, sew back (B) to front at shoulder seams.

3 Staystitch neck edge and notched edge of neck facing.

4. Clean-finish unnotched edge of neck facing (C). With right sides together, stitch neck facing to neck edge, clipping where necessary. Clip curves and trim seam. Open facing and press seam allowance toward facing. Understitch. Turn facing to inside. Press. Tack facing in place at shoulder seams and center front.

5. Staystitch armhole edges of apron.

6. Press under ¼ inch seam allowance on long unnotched edge of each sleeve cap (D). Pin notched edge to armhole edge, clipping armhole edge where necessary. Stitch. Stitch again ⅛ inch from previous stitching within the seam allowance. Clip curves and trim seam. Press seam allowance toward sleeve cap. With right sides together, pin side seams and bottom straight edges of sleeve caps. Stitch bottom of each sleeve cap and side seams in one continuous line. Fold sleeve cap in half. Cover seam allowance with folded edge of sleeve cap. Slipstitch in place.

7. Fold under ¼ inch on the long edge of the back and neck facing. Fold along fold line and stitch in place.

8. Fold under ¼ inch of hem. Fold under another ¼ inch and stitch.

Adult's/Child's Covering

For Large Doll (3 pieces; patterns on pages 63–65)
For Small Doll (patterns on pages 171)

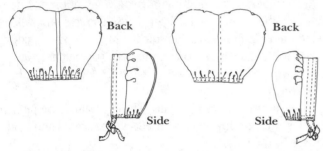

1. Press under ⅛ inch on lower, straight edge of covering (A). Fold under an additional ¼ inch. Stitch along both edges of fold to create a casing. Using a needle, insert lightweight string or heavy thread through casing. Pull string until gathered bottom edge measures 4 inches (2 inches for 12-inch doll).

2. Fold covering in half, wrong sides together. Sew along solid stitching line from top to lower dot. Seam should be pressed to form a small pleat centered over seam line. (Fold child's covering, then sew along broken stitching line from top to lower dot. Do not press open.)

3. Press under ⅛ inch on one long unnotched edge and both ends of covering brim (B). Fold under an additional ¼ inch. Stitch along hemline and ends. (Fold child's covering brim like adult's, then stitch along hemline, very close to fold. Stitch again ½ inch from fold edge; ¼ inch for 12-inch doll.)

4. Gather covering between dots. With right sides together, pin covering to covering brim, keeping brim edges even with the lower edge of the covering and the center notch of the brim at the center of the covering. Zig-zag stitch close to earlier stitching. Trim seam. Press toward covering.

5. Press under ¼ inch on the long edges and ends of the covering ties (C). Zig-zag using a very small stitch along both long edges and ends of covering ties (C). Trim away excess seam allowance in center. Cut tie in half. Tack one tie to each side of lower edge of covering.

Adult's/Child's Bonnet

For Large Doll (9 pieces; patterns on pages 67–75)
For Small Doll (patterns on pages 173–75)

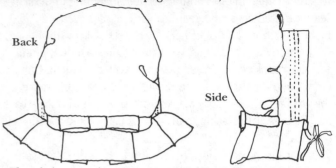

1. Place brim covering (D) around cardboard brim (B) with fold at front of brim. Top-stitch 1 inch from fold, keeping fabric stretched and tight. Top-stitch again, ⅜ inch from previous stitching, again keeping fabric stretched. Top-stitch a third time, ⅜ inch from previous stitching, again keeping fabric stretched. Top-stitch a fourth time, ⅜ inch from previous stitching, as instructed before.

For 12-inch doll, top-stitch ½ inch from fold. Top-stitch again ⅛ inch from previous stitching. Repeat to create three lines of top-stitching.

2. Apply interfacing to wrong side of one bonnet piece (A). With wrong sides together, stitch bonnet ¼ inch from raw edges. Pleat curved edge between dots, making approximately ¼ inch pleats. Curve should measure 12¼–12½ inches total from edge to edge, 7–7¼ inches for 12-inch doll, when pleating is finished. Stitch across top of pleats with ¼-inch seam.

3. Stitch bonnet to brim on stitching line, using ⅜-inch seam. Turn raw edges of brim under toward raw edges of bonnet. Stitch ⅛ inch from edge. Turn bonnet rightside out.

4. Fold flap (E) in half, right sides together. Stitch ends ¼ inch from edge. Trim seam, clip corner, turn rightside out, and press. Make darts in flap. Press toward center. Make pleats in *flap* by folding on solid line and bringing it to the dotted line (on right side of fabric). Stitch in place with ¼-inch seam.

Make pleats in *bonnet* by folding on solid line and bringing it to the dotted line. Stitch pleats in place with ¼-inch seam. Pin flap to bonnet, matching pleats with pleats and darts to bonnet/brim seam. Stitch allowing ¼-inch seam. Press under ¼ inch on one long side of binding (C). Pin right side of binding strip to wrong side of flap, leaving ends extend ½ inch past brim edge. Stitch ⅜-inch seam through all thicknesses.

5. Fold ties (I) in half, right sides together, and stitch with ¼-inch seam along the long side and one end. Clip corners. Turn rightside out and press.

6. Stitch ties to brim at dots through all thicknesses. Turn in ends of binding and fold binding over raw edges. Hand-stitch.

7. Fold bow (F) along foldlines. Overlap ends and stitch through all thicknesses in center. Fold bow knot (H) around center of bow, hiding stitching. Overlap ends in back and slipstitch.

8. Press under ¼ inch on raw ends of ribbon band (G).

Center bow on ribbon band and tack in place. Slipstitch ends of ribbon band to bonnet at brim/bonnet seam, centering dots at brim/flap seam. Tack band to bonnet and flap at pleats.

Adult's/Child's Slip

For Large Doll (4 pieces; patterns on pages 77–83)
For Small Doll (patterns on pages 77–79)

Front

1. With right sides together, stitch slip front (A) to slip back (B) at side seams.
2. Clean-finish lower unnotched edge of slip facing front (C) and back (D).
3. With right sides together, stitch facing front to facing back at side seams.
4. With right sides together, pin facings to slip. Stitch continuously around armholes, across shoulders and around neck edges. Clip and trim seams. Turn facing to inside. Press.
5. To form tucks around the lower edge of the slip, bring dotted lines to meet solid lines on right side. Stitch.
6. Make buttonholes on slip's front straps. Attach buttons on slip's back straps.
7. Make a tiny bow of ¼-inch ribbon, ⅛-inch for 12-inch doll, and attach center front.

Adult's/Child's Nightgown

For Large Doll (7 pieces; patterns on pages 85–95)
For Small Doll (patterns on pages 181–83)

Front

Back

1. Staystitch neck edges of bodice front (A) and bodice back (B).
2. With right sides together, stitch front to back at shoulder seams. Press seams open.
3. With wrong sides together, fold ruffle (C) in half lengthwise. Baste. Gather along raw edge of ruffle. With right sides together, pin ruffle to neck edge, keeping tapered ends of ruffle even with fold lines on bodice fronts. Distribute fullness evenly. Baste ruffle to neck edge.
4. Clean-finish long unnotched edge of neck facing (D). With right sides together, pin facing to neck edge, keeping ruffle between bodice and neck facing. Stitch through all thick-

nesses. Open facing. Clip curves. Trim seam. Press seam toward facing. Understitch. Turn facing to inside. Press. Tack facing at shoulder seams.
5. Gather nightgown skirt back between notches. With right sides together, stitch bodice to skirt back (E).
6. Gather nightgown skirt fronts (F) between notches. With right sides together, stitch bodice to skirt fronts.
7. Turn under ¼ inch on bottom edge of sleeves (G). Fold each sleeve edge to form a 1-inch hem. Stitch along top edge of hem. Stitch again ⅜ inch from top edge of hem to form casing for elastic. Cut a 5-inch piece of ¼-inch elastic for each sleeve, 2½-inch piece for 12-inch doll. Pull elastic through casing. Tack elastic at both ends of sleeve casing.
8. Gather top edge of sleeve between notches. With right sides together, pin sleeve in armhole opening, matching notches and keeping dot at shoulder seam. Stitch. Stitch again within the seam allowance, ⅛ inch from previous stitching. Trim seam.
9. With right sides together, pin nightgown together at sides and sleeve seams. Stitch sleeve seams and side seams in a continuous seam, having sleeve hems even and matching underarm seams.
10. Clean-finish front extensions and front edge of neck facing.
11. With right sides together, stitch center front seam from bottom edge to lower edge of extension. Pivot at corner of extension and stitch across lower edge of extension. Clip diagonally to corner of extension. Press seam open below extension. Fold extension to inside along fold line on right side of front.
12. Fold under ¼ inch on bottom edge of nightgown. Fold under another ¼ inch and stitch to form hem.
13. Make buttonholes on right side of front. Sew buttons on front left.

Adult's/Child's Panties

For Large Doll (1 piece; pattern on pages 97–99)
For Small Doll (pattern on page 185)

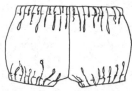

1. With right sides together, stitch panties together at center front and center back seams matching double and triple notches.
2. Fold under ¼ inch on top edge of panties. Fold under another ½ inch and stitch to form casing, leaving a small opening to insert elastic.
3. Cut a 13-inch length of ¼-inch elastic, 7½-inch length for 12-inch doll. Insert through waistline casing. Stitch ends of elastic together and close seam opening.
4. With right sides together, stitch inner leg seams of panties, matching notches and center seams.
5. Fold under ¼ inch on bottom of each panty leg. Fold each

under another ½ inch and then stitch to form casing leaving a small opening to insert elastic. Cut two 8½-inch lengths of elastic, two 4¼-inch lengths for 12-inch doll, and insert one in each leg casing. Stitch ends of elastic together and close seam opening.

Adult's/Child's Shoes

For Large Doll (3 pieces; patterns on page 101)
For Small Doll (patterns on page 187)

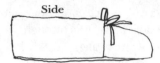

1. With right sides together, fold shoe-back piece (A) together lengthwise. Stitch ends. Trim seams. Turn rightside out. Press. Staystitch along open edge of shoe back forming a ¼-inch seam allowance. Clip seam.
2. With right sides together, pin shoe back to sole (B), matching center dots and edges of shoe back with X's on sole. Stitch.
3. Turn under ⅛ inch on straight edge of shoe top (C). Turn under another ¼ inch and stitch. With right sides together, pin shoe top to front of sole, matching center dots and overlapping sides of shoe top on shoe back. Stitch. Turn shoe rightside out.
4. Cut four, 6-inch lengths of ⅛-inch ribbon. Tack ribbon to upper edges of shoe back.

Adult's Shirt

For Large Doll (5 pieces; patterns on pages 103–107)
For Small Doll (patterns on pages 189–91)

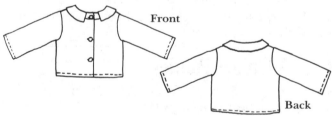

1. With right sides together, stitch fronts (A) to back (B) at shoulder seams. Staystitch neck edge. Clean-finish front edges of shirt. Turn to inside along fold lines. Baste along top and bottom edge of fold.
2. Apply interfacing to the wrong side of one collar section (C). With right sides together, stitch collar together at ends and notched edge. Trim seams and clip corners. Turn collar rightside out. Press. Baste together along lower notched edge.
3. Staystitch both collar band pieces (D) along notched edges. With right sides together, pin collar to one collar band section matching notches and clipping where necessary. Ends of collar should come to dots on collar band. Baste. Press under ¼ inch on unnotched edge of remaining collar band. With right sides together, pin collar band pieces together with collar sandwiched between. Stitch ends and notched edge through all thicknesses. Trim seam and clip curves. Turn collar band rightside out.

4. With right sides together, pin unpressed collar band to neck edge of shirt, matching center dots and having shoulder seams at remaining dots. Stitch. Trim and clip seam. Press seam toward collar band. Bring remaining collar band over seam allowance and slipstitch in place.
5. Fold under ¼ inch on bottom edge of each sleeve (E). Fold under another ¼ inch and stitch. With right sides together, pin sleeve to armhole opening matching notches. Stitch. Stitch again, ⅛ inch from previous stitching within seam allowance. Trim seam. With right sides together, pin each sleeve and adjacent side of the shirt body together, matching underarm seams. Stitch each sleeve and adjacent side seam of shirt in one continuous seam.
6. Fold under ¼ inch on bottom edge of shirt. Fold under another ¼ inch and stitch.
7. Make buttonholes and attach buttons.

Child's Shirt

For Large Doll (4 pieces; patterns on pages 109–113)
For Small Doll (patterns on pages 193)

1. Apply interfacing to wrong side of one collar section (C).
2. With right sides together, sew collar sections together along unnotched edge and ends. Clip curves and trim seam. Turn rightside out and press.
3. Sew front (A) to back (B) at shoulders.
4. Turn hem of sleeves under ¼ inch and then another ¼ inch. Stitch. With right sides together, pin sleeve to armhole opening, matching notches. Stitch. Stitch again ⅛ inch from previous stitching within seam allowance. Trim seam. With right sides together, pin each sleeve and adjacent side of the shirt body together, matching underarm seams. Stitch each sleeve and adjacent side seam of shirt in one continuous seam.
5. Staystitch neck of shirt.
6. Sew collar to shirt with un-interfaced side of collar next to right side of shirt, ending collar at dot. Clip curves. Understitch collar.
7. Clean-finish long edge of shirt front. Fold shirt along fold line with right sides together. Stitch along neck edge to dot. Clip corners, trim, and turn facing.
8. Fold under ¼ inch on bottom edge of shirt. Fold another ¼ inch and stitch.
9. Make buttonholes and attach buttons.

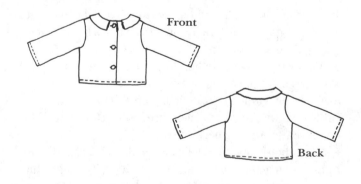

Adult's Plain Coat

For Large Doll (7 pieces; patterns on pages 115–21)
For Small Doll (patterns on pages 195–97)

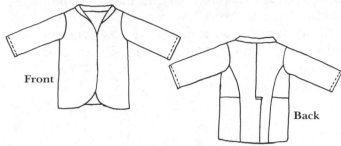

Front

Back

1. With right sides together, stitch side top (A) to side bottom (B), matching notches. Press seams open.
2. With right sides together, stitch center seam of back (C) to small dot. Clip to dot. Press seam open.
3. With right sides together, stitch side section (A/B) to back (C), matching notches and clipping curve as necessary to fit. Press seam toward center.
4. With right sides together, stitch front (D) to side (A/B) at side seams and shoulder seams, matching notches. Press seams open.
5. Apply interfacing to wrong side of collar (E).
6. With right sides together, pin notched edge of collar to neck edge, matching notches. Sew. Clip curves.
7. Apply interfacing to wrong side of facing (F).
8. With right sides together, sew notched edges of facing (F) together. Press seam open. Clean-finish inner edge of facing.
9. With right sides together, pin facing to coat. Sew continuously around to back flap. Stitch ends of facing to flap. Clip curves and corners. Turn facing to inside and tack into place at shoulder seams, center back seam, and side seams.
10. Bring left flap to outside so it extends ½ inch from center back seam. Turn top edge of flap under ¼ inch and edge-stitch horizontally close to fold.
11. Turn sleeves (G) under ¼″ along unnotched edge. Turn under another ¼ inch and stitch.
12. With right sides together, sew sleeve seam, matching notches.
13. With right sides together, set sleeves into coat, matching notches. Stitch seam and then sew again ⅛″ from previous stitching within seam allowance. Trim seam.
14. Attach four hook and eye closures inside coat front.

Child's Plain Coat

For Large Doll (5 pieces; patterns on pages 123–29)
For Small Doll (patterns on pages 199–201)

1. With right sides together, stitch center back seam of coat back (B), matching notches.
2. With right sides together, pin coat front (A) to back at curved edge. Clip curves as necessary to fit. Stitch. Press seams toward back.
3. With rights sides together, sew front and back together at

the shoulders, matching notches.
4. Staystitch neck edge.
5. Apply interfacing to the wrong side of facing (D) and clean-finish inner edge. With right sides together, pin facing to coat. Sew a continuous seam around outer edge. Clip curves, trim seam, and turn the facing to the inside of the coat. Press.
6. Apply interfacing to the wrong side of one collar (C).
7. Press under ¼ inch on notched edge of un-interfaced collar.
8. With right sides together, pin collar pieces together. Sew along ends and unnotched edge. Clip curves and trim seam. Turn rightside out and press.
9. With right sides together, pin interfaced side of collar to right side of coat, matching notches. Collar edge should meet edge of coat. Clip curves as necessary and then sew. Trim seam and press toward collar. Slipstitch un-interfaced collar piece over seam.
10. Turn under ¼ inch on bottom edge of each sleeve (E). Turn under another ¼ inch and sew.
11. With right sides together, sew sleeve seam, matching notches.
12. With right sides together, set sleeves into coat, matching notches and seams. Sew seam and then sew again, ⅛ inch from previous seam within seam allowance. Trim seam.
13. Attach four hook and eye closures to inside of coat.

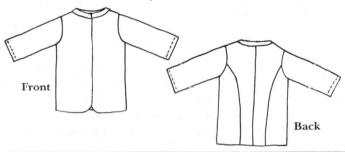

Front

Back

Adult's/Child's Pants

For Large Doll (4 pieces; patterns on pages 131–35)
For Small Doll (patterns on page 203)

Front

Back

1. Clean-finish curved, dotted edge of front pocket (A) and back pocket (C).
2. With right sides together, stitch each front pocket to pants front (B), matching notches. Trim seams and clip curves. Turn pocket to the inside of the pants with right sides out. Machine-baste each pocket to pants at sides and top.
3. With right sides together, pin back pocket to pants back (D). Stitch to dot.

4. With right sides together, stitch front sections together along unnotched edge. Do the same for back sections (D). Clip curves and press seams open.

5. With right sides together, pin side seams, matching notches. Sandwich front between back pocket and pants back, placing top edge of front at side dot. Sew front and back pocket sections together from pocket dot to side. Starting at side dot stitch through all thicknesses to lower edge.

6. Turn under ¼ inch on pants bottom. Turn under another ¼ inch and stitch.

7. Turn under ¼ inch on top of pants. Turn under another ¼ inch and stitch.

8. With right sides together, stitch inner leg seams, matching notches.

9. Sew buttonholes and attach buttons.

10. Use ½-inch black elastic for suspenders, ¼-inch for 12-inch doll. Tack suspenders at dots on pants back. Cross suspenders to form an X on back and pull snugly over shoulders. Tack in front.

Adult's/Child's Vest

For Large Doll (3 pieces; patterns on page 137)
For Small Doll (patterns on page 205)

Front   Back

1. Press under ¼ inch on both long edges of vest band (A). Fold band in half lengthwise and stitch very close to edge.

2. Baste vest band to right side of one vest back (B), placing ends of band even with raw edges between dots.

3. Sew vest backs (B) to vest fronts (C) at shoulder seams. Press seams open.

4. With right sides together, pin one front/back vest unit to the other front/back unit. Stitch all seams except side seams. Trim seams and corners. Clip curves.

5. Turn vest rightside out through one side opening. Vest band will be on the right side of the vest. Press.

6. To finish side seams, bring right sides together. Stitch seam through three thicknesses leaving the one inner seam allowance free. Fold free seam allowance under. Press stitched seam allowances toward folded seam allowance. Bring folded seam allowance over the stitched seam to cover all raw edges. Slipstitch in place.

7. Tack vest band to vest at squares.

8. Hooks and eyes are used as vest closures. Attach on inside edge so they are invisible from outside.

Adult's/Child's Hat

For Large Doll (3 pieces; patterns on pages 139–41)
For Small Doll (patterns on page 207)

1. Apply interfacing hat top (A) pieces, hat brim (C) pieces, and one hat side (B) piece.

2. With interfaced sides together, sew around raw edge of top hat with a zig-zag stitch.

3. With right sides together, sew ends of interfaced hat side (B) together, matching notches. Repeat this step for un-interfaced hat side. Press seams open.

4. Pin interfaced hat side to hat top, matching seam with dot and matching other dots. Clip edge of hat side as necessary to ease fitting. Sew.

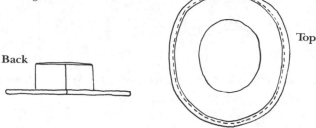

Back   Top

5. Press under ¼ inch on one long side of un-interfaced hat side.

6. Pin right side of un-interfaced hat side to wrong side of hat top, matching seam with dot and matching other dots. Clip as necessary to ease fitting. Sew seam on top of previous stitching as outlined in step #4 above.

7. Trim seam and turn inside out, so that right sides of both hat sides (B) are out. Right side of interfaced hat side should be on the outside of the hat and un-interfaced hat side should be on the inside. This is the hat body.

8. Pin one fold of wide, black bias tape ⅜ inch from raw edge of one interfaced hat brim (C).

9. With interfaced sides together, sew around inner circle of hat brim (C), using a zig-zag stitch.

10. Pin hat brim to hat body using bias tape. Pin side of brim next to the interfaced side of hat body, matching dots. Clip curves of hat body as necessary to ease fitting. Sew, being careful not to catch un-interfaced hat side. Sew again on top of previous stitching. Trim seam and press up toward hat top. Slipstitch un-interfaced hat side to brim, hiding seam.

11. Cut a hat brim out of medium lightweight cardboard, following cardboard cutting line on hat brim pattern. Sandwich cardboard between interfaced sections of hat brim. Cardboard should fit snugly but smoothly at inner circle. If it doesn't, remove it and trim it to fit.

12. Stretch bias tape around to bottom side of hat brim. Pin tape in place and slipstitch it to bottom fabric. On top side of brim, edge-stitch on bias tape close to the seam.

13. Cut a 16½-inch length of ⅝-inch black ribbon, 8¼-inch length of ¼-inch ribbon for 12-inch doll. Place ribbon around hat at base of hat body. Fasten the ends together at center of left side. Tack ribbon to hat at several spots to hold it in place.

14. To make the bow for the side of the hat, cut a 7-inch length of ⅝-inch black ribbon, 3½-inch length of ¼-inch ribbon for 12-inch doll. Fold ribbon to make a 3¼-inch loop (1⅝-inch for 12-inch doll). Fasten ends at the center. Cut a 1¾-inch piece of ⅝-inch black ribbon (⅞-inch of ¼-inch ribbon for 12-inch doll) and place it vertically around previous 3¼-inch (1⅝-inch) loop, in the center, covering ends of loop.

Tack small loop in place with raw ends at back of bow.

15. Attach bow to ribbon band around hat at left side where raw ends have been fastened. Tack it in place over the raw ends. Tack bow down in several places to secure it.

Adult's/Child's Nightshirt

For Large Doll (4 pieces; patterns on pages 143–49)
For Small Doll (patterns on pages 209–211)

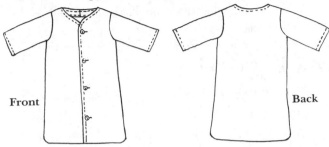

Front   Back

1. With right sides together, stitch facings (C) together at center back. Clean-finish long unnotched edge of facing.
2. With right sides together, stitch fronts (A) to back (B) at shoulder seams.
3. With right sides together, pin facing to neck and front edges. Stitch. Trim seam and clip curves. Press facing to inside. On outside, topstitch fronts and neck edge.
4. Gather top edges of sleeves (D) between notches. With rights sides together, pin sleeves to armhole openings, matching notches and easing in fullness. Stitch. Turn under ¼ inch on bottom edges of sleeves. Turn under another ¼ inch and stitch to form sleeve hems.
5. With right sides together, pin front and back together at side seams. Pin sleeves together, matching underarm seams and edges of sleeve hems. Stitch sleeves and sides in one continuous seam, stopping at dots at lower edges of sides.
6. Make buttonholes and sew on buttons.
7. Slipstitch hem using a very narrow seam allowance. Taper to nothing where curves meet side seams.

Adult's/Child's Boxer Shorts

For Large Doll (1 piece; pattern on pages 97–99)
For Small Doll (patterns on page 185)

1. With right sides together, stitch shorts together at center front and center back seams matching double and triple notches.
2. Fold under ¼ inch on top edge of panties. Fold under another ½ inch and stitch to form casing, leaving a small opening to insert elastic.
3. Cut a 13-inch length of ¼-inch elastic, 6½-inch length for 12-inch doll. Insert through waistline casing. Stitch ends of elastic together and close seam opening.

4. With right sides together, stitch inner leg seam of shorts, matching notches and center seams.
5. Fold under ¼ inch on each leg of shorts. Fold under another ¼ inch and stitch to form hem.

Mini Doll

(All patterns for mini-doll and mini-doll clothing on pages 211–13)

Front   Back

Front   Back

Note: Many of the pieces for this doll are quite small and seam allowances are only ⅛ inch. Because of the pieces' sizes and their narrow seam allowances, much of the sewing is most easily done by hand. Machine-stitching is recommended for the doll body and longer expanses of stitching. Whichever method is used, stitches must be tiny and tight.

Doll Body *(1 piece)*

1. With right sides together, stitch body front (A) to back, leaving seam open between dots. Clip all curves, paying special attention to underarms, neck and crotch.
2. Turn body rightside out using crotchet hook or some other blunt object to assist in turning.
3. Stuff body, making sure that stuffing reaches to all extremities. Slipstitch opening between dots.

Dress *(1 piece)*

1. Press under ⅛ inch on neck edge, bottom of sleeves and lower edge of dress (A). Fold under another ⅛ inch and stitch.

2. With right sides together, stitch front to back. Clip diagonally to stitching at underarms. Turn dress rightside out.

3. Put dress on doll. Using a double strand of thread, make small running stitches along neck edge of dress. Pull to gather dress snugly around neck. Tack thread securely.

Apron *(2 pieces)*

1. Press under ⅛ inch on lower edge and sides of apron (A). Fold under another ⅛ inch and stitch. Gather along upper edge to measure 1¾ inches.

2. Press under ⅛ inch on both long edges of apron belt (B). Fold in ⅛ inch along ends of belt. Fold in another ⅛ inch and stitch.

3. Fold belt in half lengthwise along fold line. Center gathered apron in apron belt. Sandwich apron within fold of apron belt. Stitch belt together, catching apron at same time.

4. Put apron on doll. Pull apron snugly around doll's waist. Overlap apron belt in back and tack in place.

Bonnet *(3 pieces)*

1. With right sides together, stitch bonnet brim pieces (A) together along curved edge. Clip curves. Turn rightside out. Press.

2. Gather bonnet (B) section along curved edge.

3. With right sides together, stitch bonnet brim to bonnet, having edges of bonnet brim even with lower edge of bonnet. Turn rightside out.

4. With right sides together, fold bonnet band (C) along fold line. Stitch ends. Turn rightside out.

5. With right sides together, stitch bonnet band to lower edge of bonnet. Press band down.

6. Using a double strand of thread, make small running stitches just above bonnet band. Pull to gather bonnet slightly along back. Tack thread securely.

7. Cut 3-inch lengths of 1/16-inch ribbon. Tack one length of ribbon to each edge of bonnet. Tie bonnet securely at doll's neck.

Shirt *(1 piece)*

1. Press under ⅛ inch on shirt (A) neck edge and bottom edge of sleeves. Fold under another ⅛ inch and stitch. With right sides together, stitch shirt front to shirt back. Clip diagonally to point at underarm seams. Turn shirt rightside out.

2. Put shirt on doll body. Using a double strand of thread, make small running stitches around neck edge of shirt. Pull to gather shirt snugly around doll neck. Tack thread securely.

Pants *(1 piece)*

1. Press under ⅛ inch on both the waist edge and bottom edge of pant (A) legs. Fold each under another ⅛ inch and stitch.

2. With right sides together, stitch pants front to pants back. Clip to point at crotch. Turn pants rightside out.

3. Cut lengths of ⅛-inch ribbon to use as suspenders. Tack suspenders in place at front and back of doll forming an X on doll back.

4. Using a double strand of thread, make small running

stitches along waist edge of pants. Pull to gather pants snugly around doll waist. Tack thread securely.

Hat *(3 pieces)*

1. Bring ends of hat band (A) together and overlap ⅛ inch to create an oval. Overcast seam on right side.

2. Place hat top (B) over hat band matching dot and seam. Using an overcast stitch, sew top to hat band.

3. With right sides together, stitch hat brim (C) to lower edges of hat band, matching dot with seam. Place hat on doll head with seam to back.

Lizzie Lapp Doll

(5 pieces; patterns on pages 213–15)

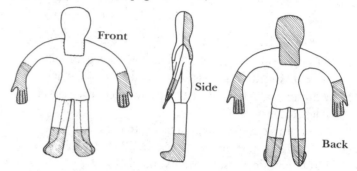

1. With right sides together, sew doll body (A) together, leaving open both the arm ends and the bottom of the body. Stitch again over previous stitching. Clip curves and trim seam. Turn the body rightside out.

2. Put some stuffing into the head and then insert a 7-inch long dowel rod into the body. Stuff the body firmly, keeping the rod centered and straight. (The rod will prevent a floppy body from developing after years of hard play.)

3. With right sides together, sew two denim hand sections (B) together, leaving the tops open for stuffing. Clip curves and corner between thumb and fingers. Trim seam and turn rightside out. First stuff thumb and fingers loosely and then do the rest of the hand. Repeat this procedure for the second hand.

4. In the center of the hand section, sew a seam from the end of the hand to the thumb joint. Sew two more seams, the same way, one on either side of this seam to create the appearance of four fingers. Repeat procedure for second hand.

5. Turn raw edge of each hand under ¼ inch and position the hands on the stuffed arms ¼ inch from edge, with thumbs away from the body. Handsew hands to arms.

6. With right sides together, sew muslin leg (C) to denim foot (D) along notched edge. Then, with right sides together, sew the two leg/foot combinations together. Stitch again over previous stitching. Clip curves and trim seam. Turn leg/foot rightside out. Repeat instructions for second leg. Stuff legs with stuffing.

7. Turn under ¼ inch on bottom edge of body, then position legs so that the top ¼ inch of each leg is within the body. The legs should be positioned so that the feet stick up when the doll is lying on its back. Handsew legs to body. The doll should be able to sit gracefully when finished.

8. With right sides together, sew hood (E) sections together along stitching line between dots. Clip curves and trim seam. Turn hood rightside out. Ease hood over head of the doll, with denim side toward the back for hair and muslin side toward the front for a face.

9. Turn under ¼ inch on raw edges of hood and handsew them to body.

Lizzie Lapp Dress

(7 pieces; patterns on pages 217–21)

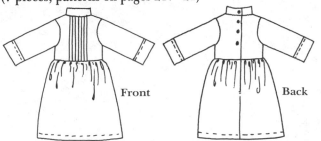

Front   Back

1. Fold bodice front (A) along fold lines. Sew ¼ inch from each fold, making two pleats. Press pleats away from center. Sew three lines of topstitching ¼ inch apart between the two pleats, as shown on pattern.

2. Press under ½ inch along fold line of each bodice back (B). Machine baste across bottom edge to secure fold in place. Sew

back and front together at shoulders and sides.

3. Turn under ¼ inch along one long edge of neckband (C). With right sides together, and raw edges even, pin neckband to neck edge of bodice. Neckband should extend ¼ inch from edge in back. Sew. Press seam toward neckband.

4. Fold neckband along fold line. Turn ends in ¼ inch so that they are even with bodice back and handsew neckband to bodice.

5. Turn under ¼ inch along unnotched edge of each sleeveband (E). With right sides together, sew sleeveband to sleeve (D), matching notches. Press seam toward sleeveband. Fold sleeveband along fold line and handsew to sleeve. On right side, edgestitch along seam.

6. With right sides together, sew sleeve seams.

7. With right sides together, pin sleeve into armhole, matching underarm seams and dot to shoulder seam.

8. With right sides together, sew center back seam of skirt back (G) to small dot.

9. With right sides together sew skirt front (F) to skirt back, matching notches. Gather top edge of skirt. With right sides together pin skirt to bodice and gather to fit. Sew.

10. Fold under ¼ inch on bottom edge of skirt. Fold under another ¼ inch and stitch to form hem.

11. Make buttonholes and attach buttons.

Yardage and Fabric Color Requirements

Fabrics and notions for each item are listed below. Suggested fabric for the doll bodies is unbleached muslin. Suggested fabric for doll clothing is cotton. Interfacing is not listed here, since in most cases only minimal amounts are needed and scraps will suffice. Lightweight interfacing is suggested where required, except for the hat and bonnet which require a heavyweight interfacing.

	20″ Doll	12″ Doll
Doll Body	½ yd. fabric, (8) 1″ buttons	¼ yd. fabric, (8) ½″ buttons
Adult Dress	⅔ yd. solid colored fabric	⅓ yd. solid colored fabric
Child's Dress	⅔ yd. solid colored fabric, (4) ½″ buttons	⅓ yd. solid colored fabric, (3) ⅜″ buttons
Adult Cape and Apron	½ yd. black fabric	¼ yd. black fabric
Child's Apron	½ yd. black fabric, (1) ⅝″ button	¼ yd. black fabric, (1) ⅜″ button
Covering	¼ yd. white organdy	⅛ yd. white organdy
Bonnet	⅔ yd. black for adult or solid colored for child's pattern	¼ yd. black for adult or solid colored for child's pattern
	⅝ yd. of 1″ satin ribbon	⅓ yd. of ½″ satin ribbon
Slip	½ yd. white fabric, (2) ⅜″ buttons	⅓ yd. white fabric, (2) 5/16″ buttons
	⅛ yd. of ¼″ satin ribbon	⅛ yd. of ⅛″ satin ribbon
Nightgown	⅔ yd. solid colored fabric, (2) ⅜″ buttons	⅓ yd. solid colored fabric, (2) ⅜″ buttons
Panties	⅓ yd. white fabric, 1 yd. ¼″ elastic	¼ yd. white fabric, ½ yd. ¼″ elastic
Boxer Shorts	⅓ yd. white fabric	¼ yd. white fabric
Shoe	⅛ yd. black fabric, ⅔ yd. ⅛″ ribbon	⅛ yd. black fabric, ½ yd. ⅛″ ribbon
Adult Shirt	⅓ yd. solid colored fabric, (5) ⅜″ buttons	¼ yd. solid colored fabric, (5) 5/16″ buttons
Child's Shirt	⅓ yd. solid colored fabric, (3) ⅜″ buttons	¼ yd. solid colored fabric, (4) 5/16″ buttons
Adult Coat	⅔ yd. black fabric, (4) hook and eye closures	¼ yd. black fabric, (4) hook and eye closures
Child's Coat	⅔ yd. black fabric, (4) hook and eye closures	¼ yd. black fabric (4) hook and eye closures
Vest	¼ yd. black fabric, (3) hook and eye closures	¼ yd. black fabric, (3) hook and eye closures
Broadfall Pants	½ yd. black fabric, (5) ⅜″ buttons	¼ yd. black fabric, (5) 5/16″ buttons
	½″ black elastic for suspenders	¼″ black elastic for suspenders
Hat	⅓ yd. black fabric, 1 yd. ⅝″ ribbon	¼ yd. black fabric, ½ yd. ¼″ ribbon
Nightshirt	½ yd. solid colored fabric, (4) ½″ buttons	¼ yd. solid colored fabric, (4) ⅜″ buttons
	Lizzie Lapp Doll	
Body	½ yd. muslin, ⅛ yd. denim	
Dress	⅓ yd. solid colored fabric (3) ⅜″ buttons	

Mini doll uses only scraps of fabric.

Patterns

The patterns in this section are given in full size. A few of the patterns extend over several pages. Remove pattern pages from book and join pattern pieces as directed along dotted lines.

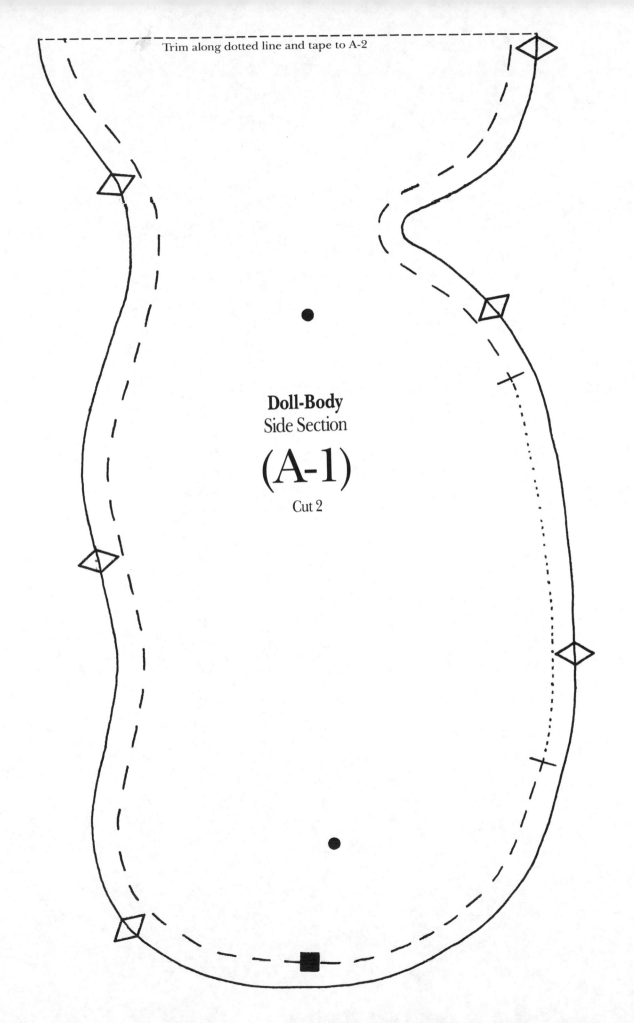

Trim along dotted line and tape to A-2

Doll-Body
Side Section

(A-1)

Cut 2

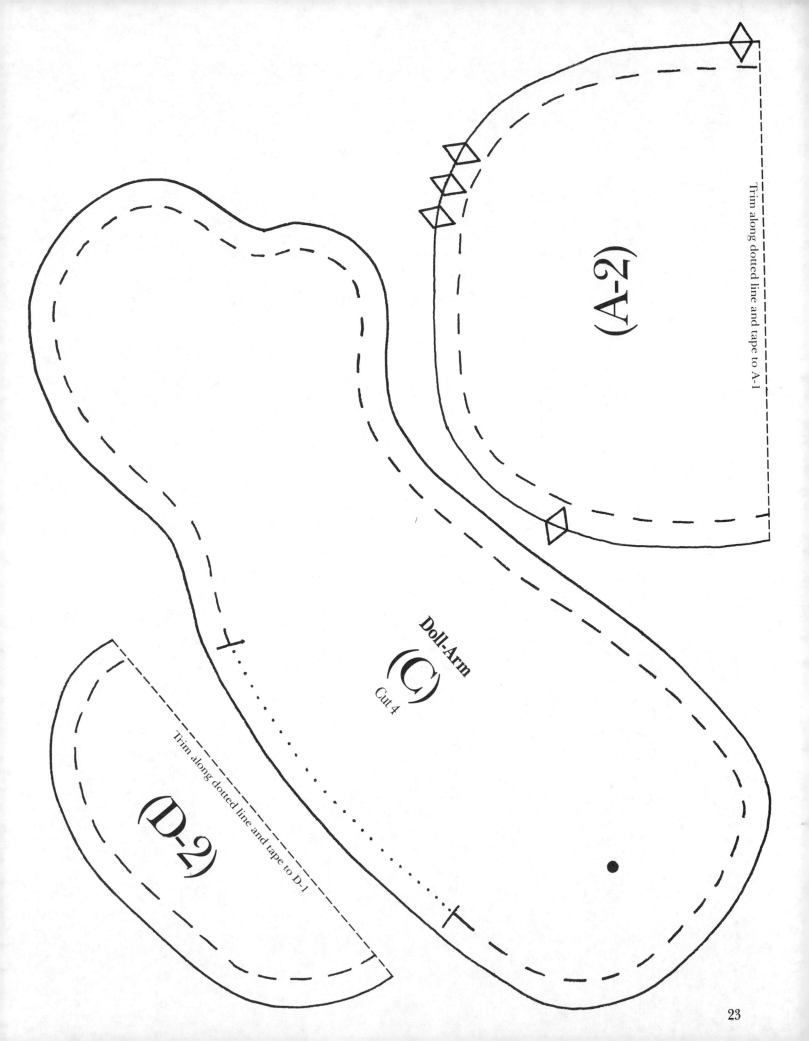

(A-2)

Trim along dotted line and tape to A-1

Doll-Arm

C

Cut 4

(D-2)

Trim along dotted line and tape to D-1

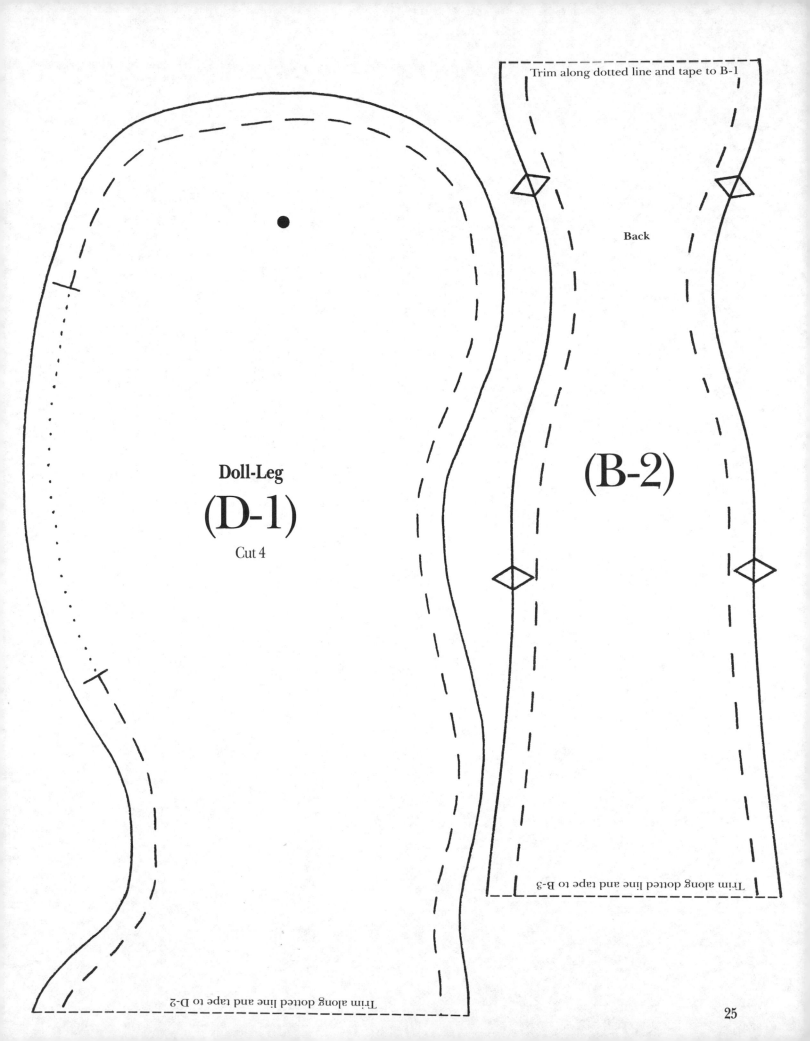

Doll-Leg

(D-1)

Cut 4

(B-2)

Trim along dotted line and tape to B-1

Back

Trim along dotted line and tape to B-3

Trim along dotted line and tape to D-2

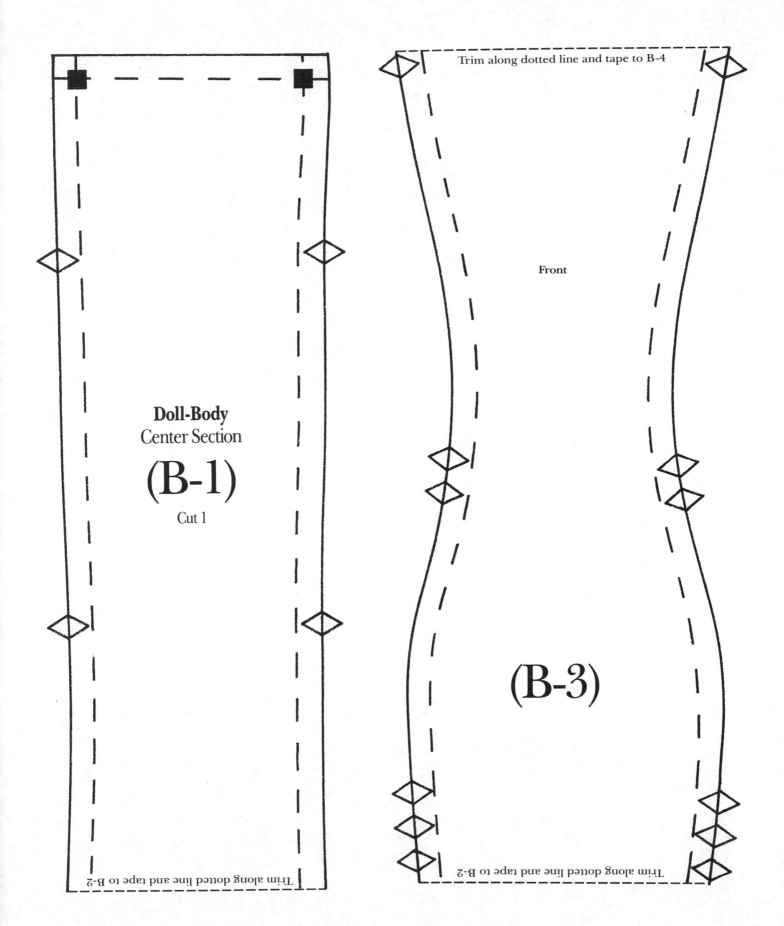

Doll-Body
Center Section
(B-1)
Cut 1

Front

(B-3)

Trim along dotted line and tape to B-4

Trim along dotted line and tape to B-2

Trim along dotted line and tape to B-2

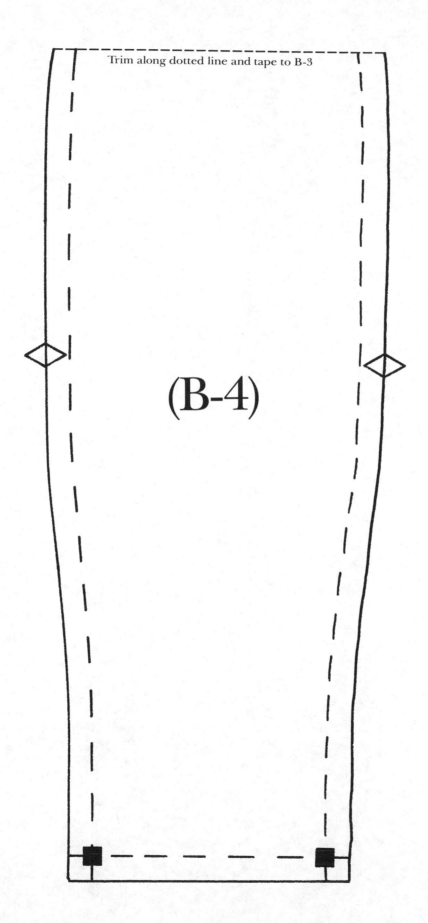

Trim along dotted line and tape to B-3

(B-4)

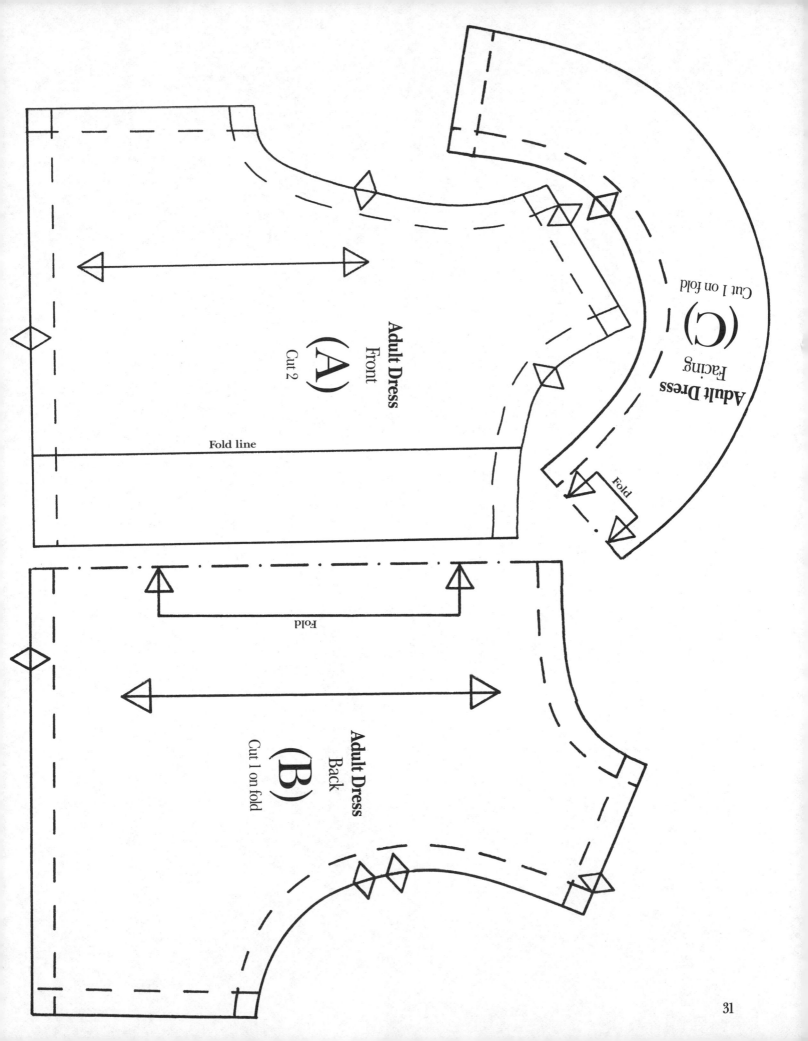

Adult Dress
Front
(A)
Cut 2

Fold line

Adult Dress
Facing
(C)
Cut 1 on fold

Fold

Adult Dress
Back
(B)
Cut 1 on fold

Fold

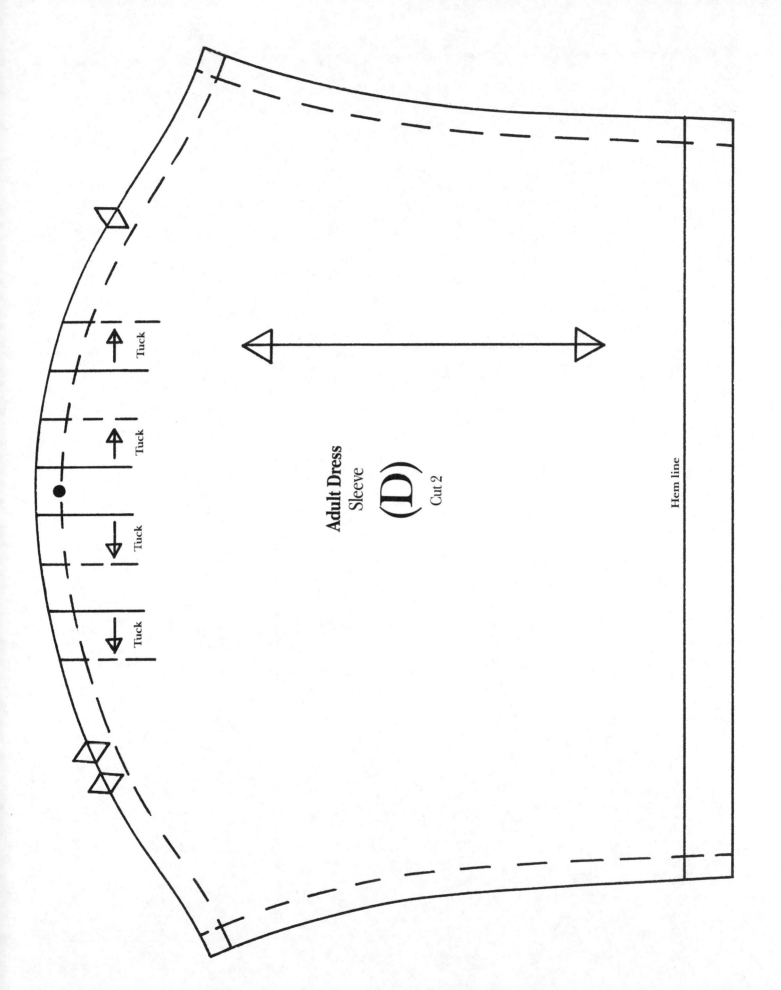

Adult Dress
Sleeve
(D)
Cut 2

Tuck

Tuck

Tuck

Tuck

Hem line

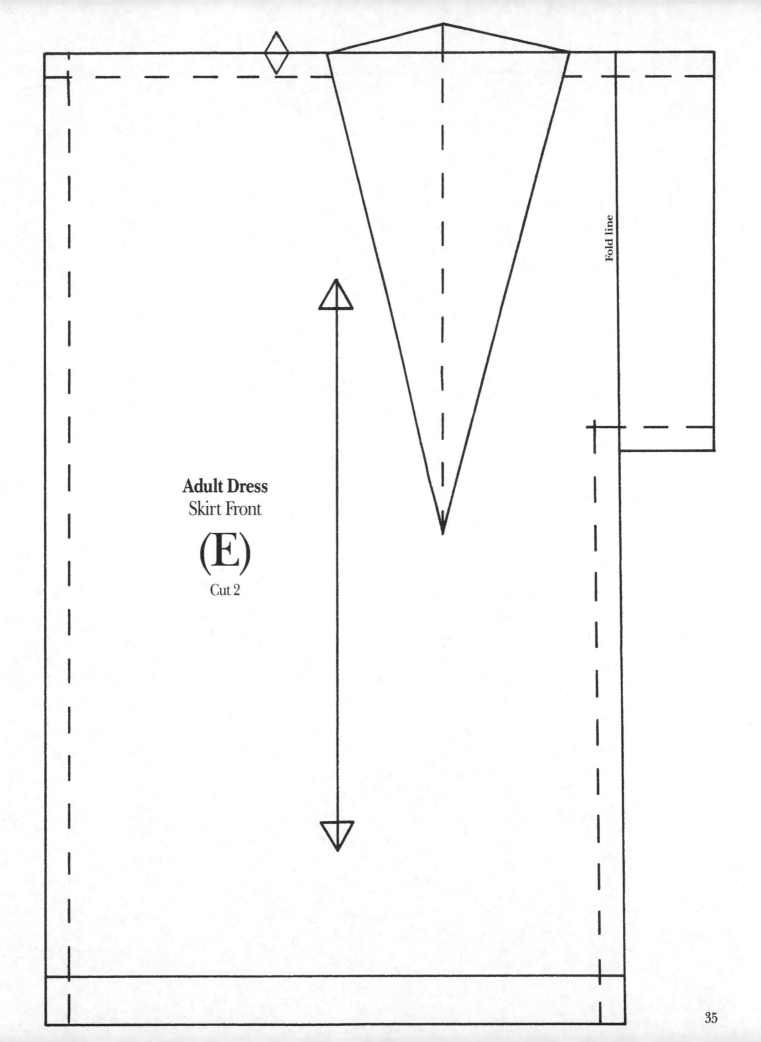

Adult Dress
Skirt Front

(E)

Cut 2

Fold line

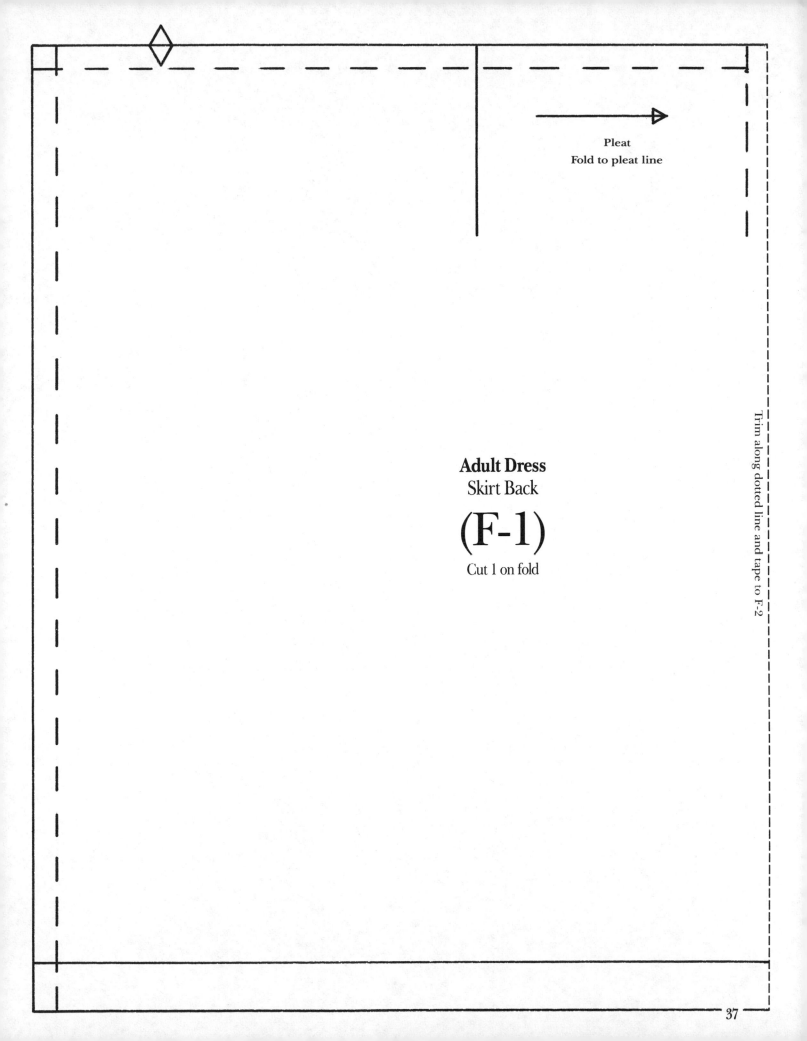

Pleat
Fold to pleat line

Adult Dress
Skirt Back

(F-1)

Cut 1 on fold

Trim along dotted line and tape to F-2

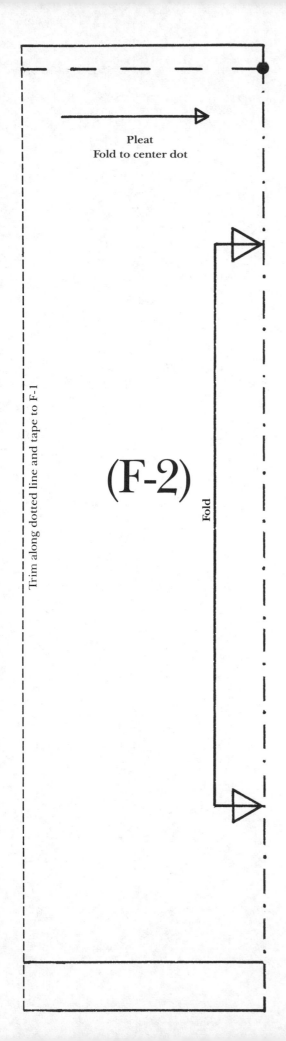

Trim along dotted line and tape to F-1

Pleat
Fold to center dot

(F-2)

Fold

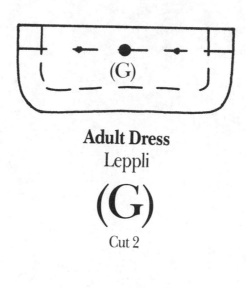

(G)

Adult Dress
Leppli

(G)

Cut 2

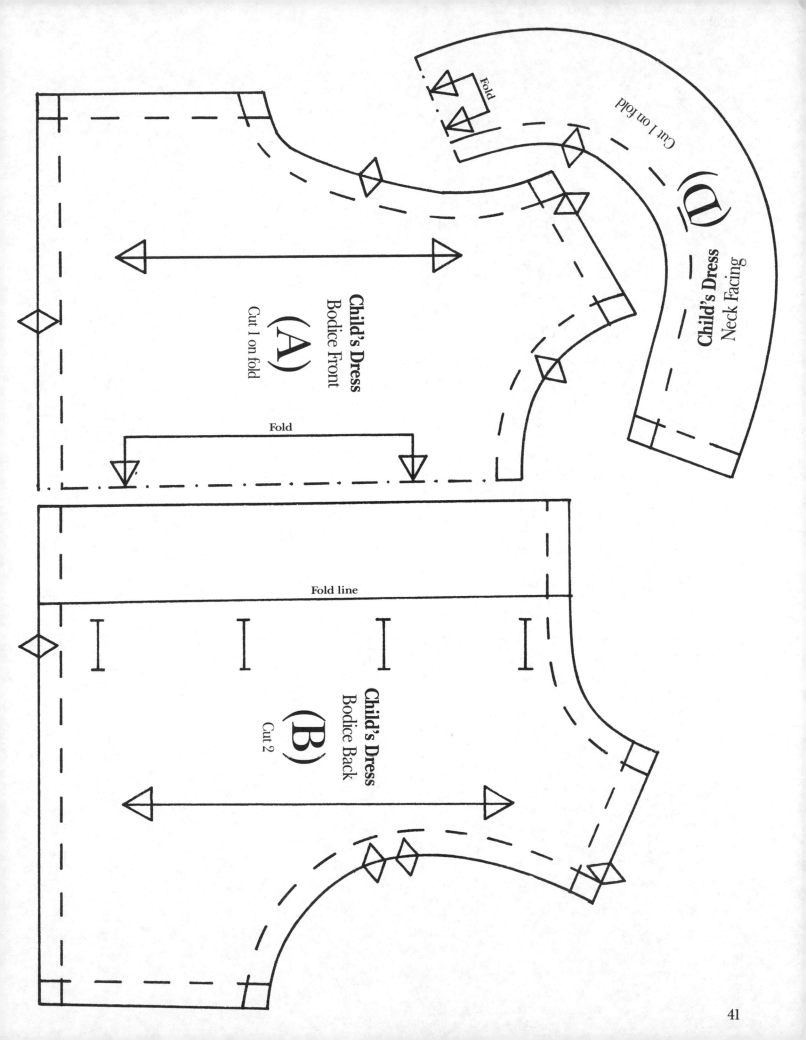

Child's Dress
Bodice Front

(A)

Cut 1 on fold

Fold

Child's Dress
Neck Facing

(D)

Cut 1 on fold

Fold

Fold line

Child's Dress
Bodice Back

(B)

Cut 2

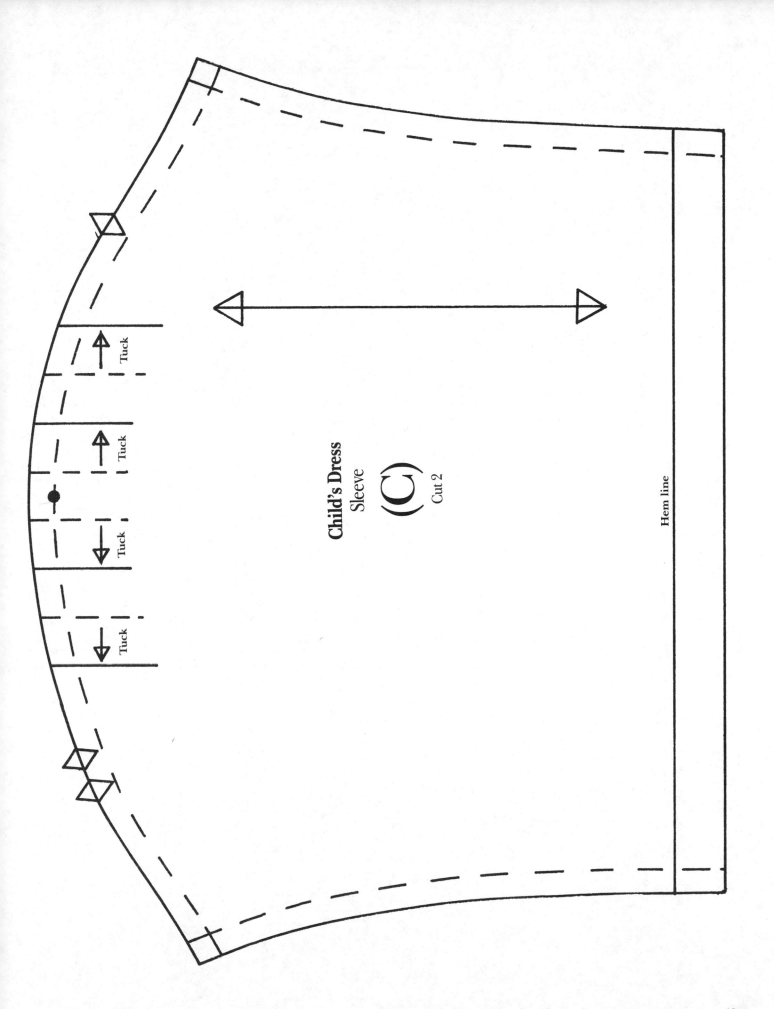

Child's Dress
Sleeve
(C)
Cut 2

Tuck
Tuck
Tuck
Tuck

Hem line

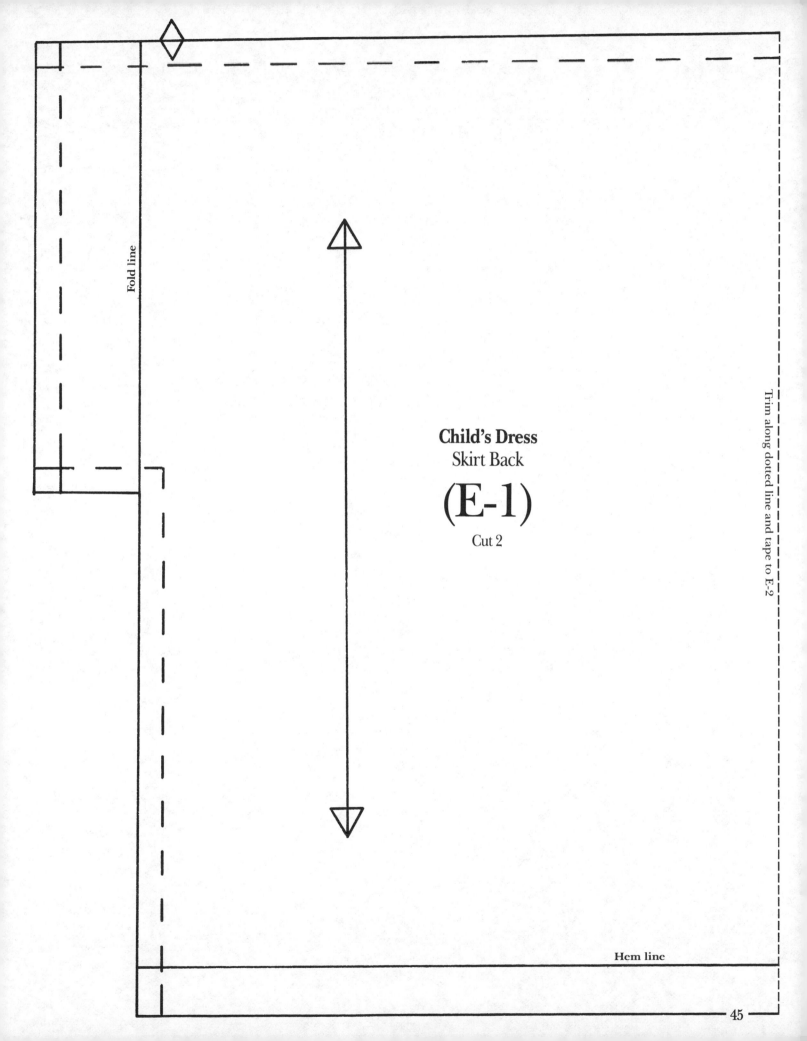

Fold line

Child's Dress
Skirt Back

(E-1)

Cut 2

Trim along dotted line and tape to E-2

Hem line

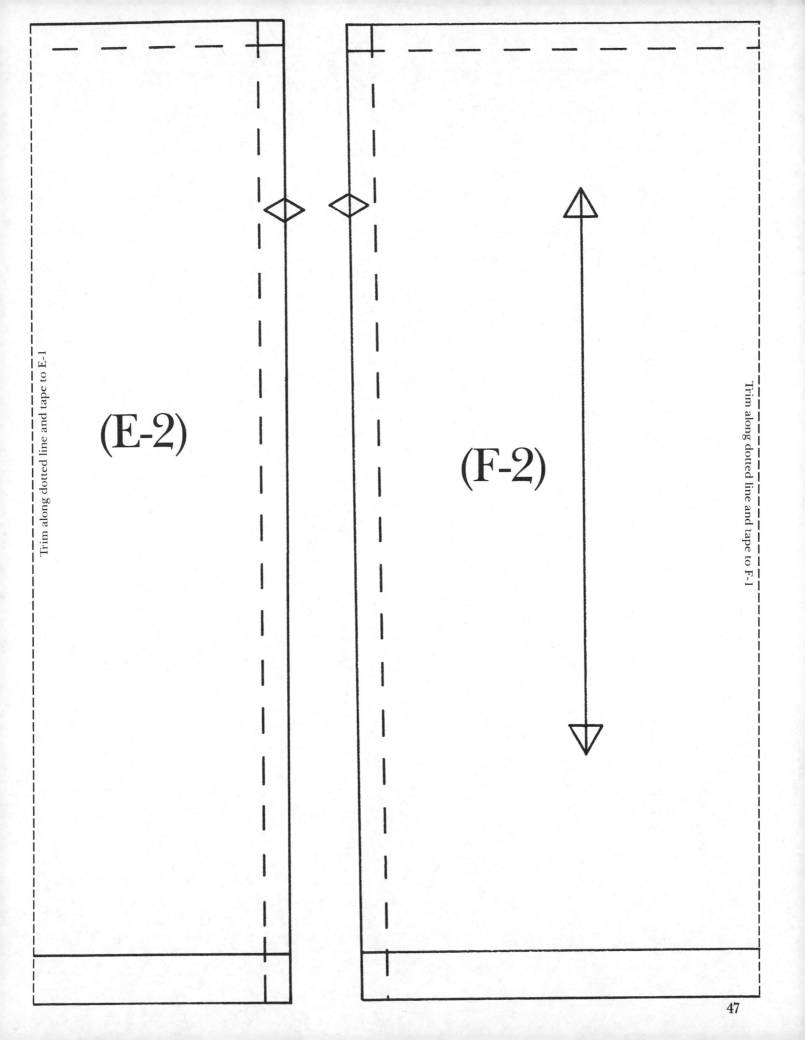

(E-2)

(F-2)

Trim along dotted line and tape to E-1

Trim along dotted line and tape to F-1

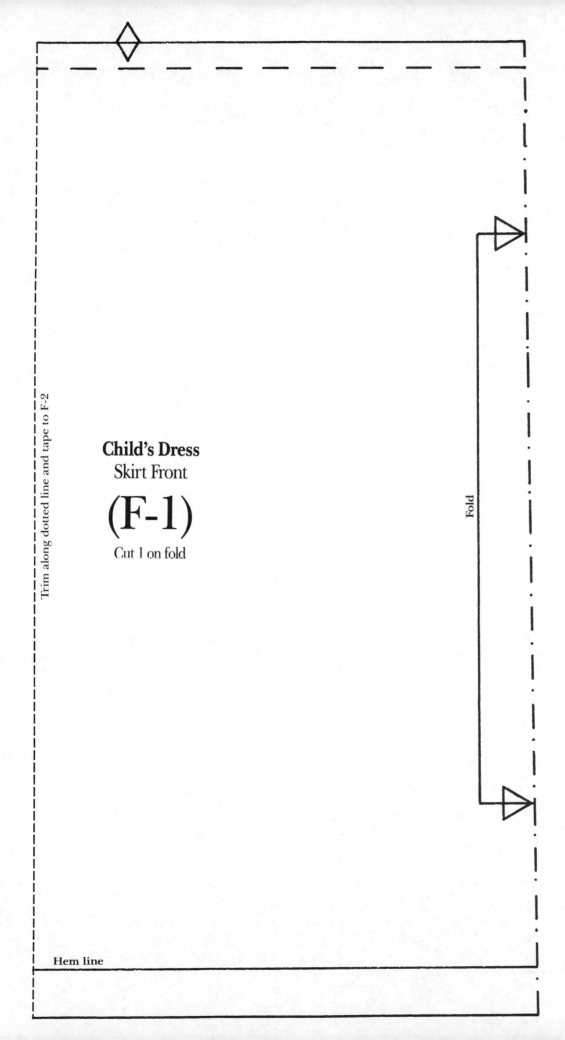

Trim along dotted line and tape to F-2

Child's Dress
Skirt Front

(F-1)

Cut 1 on fold

Fold

Hem line

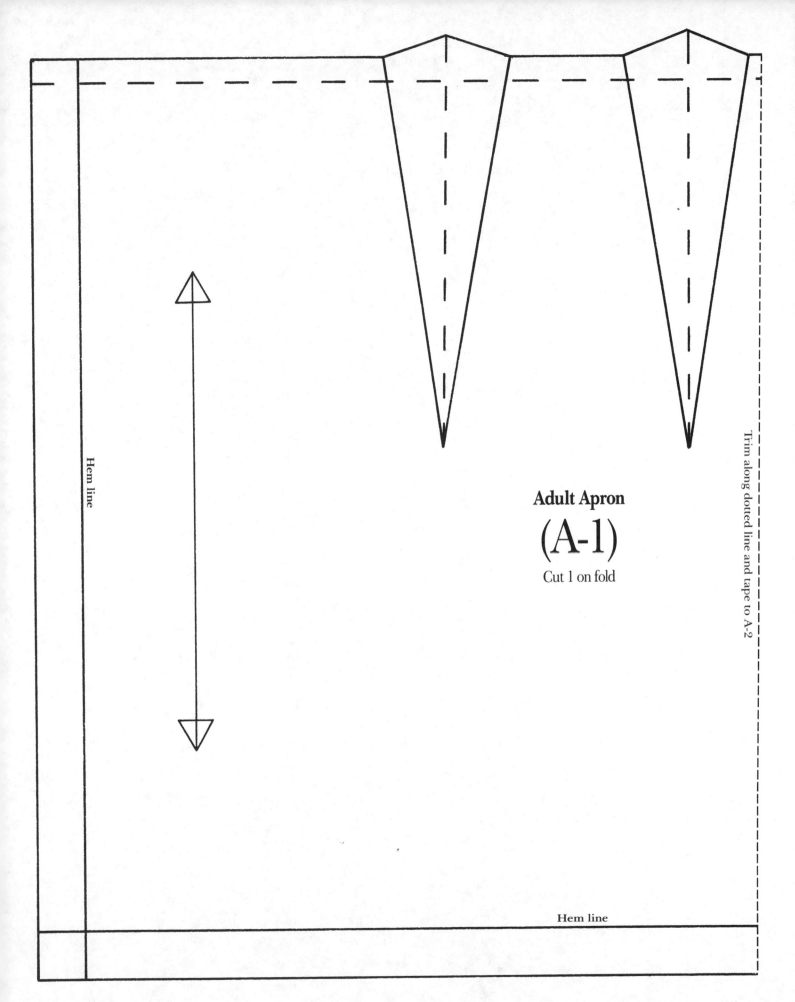

Hem line

Hem line

Adult Apron

(A-1)

Cut 1 on fold

Trim along dotted line and tape to A-2

51

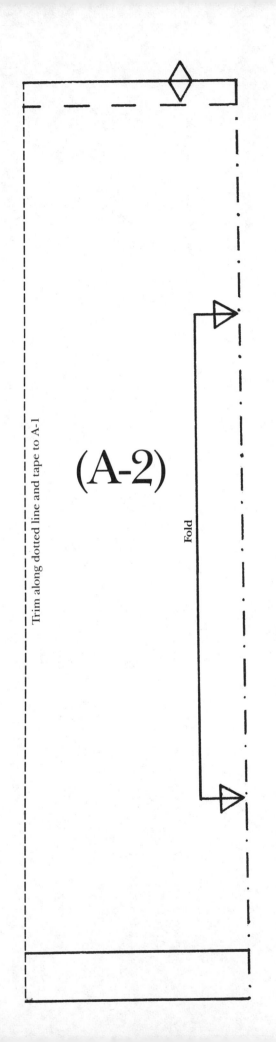

Trim along dotted line and tape to A-1

(A-2)

Fold

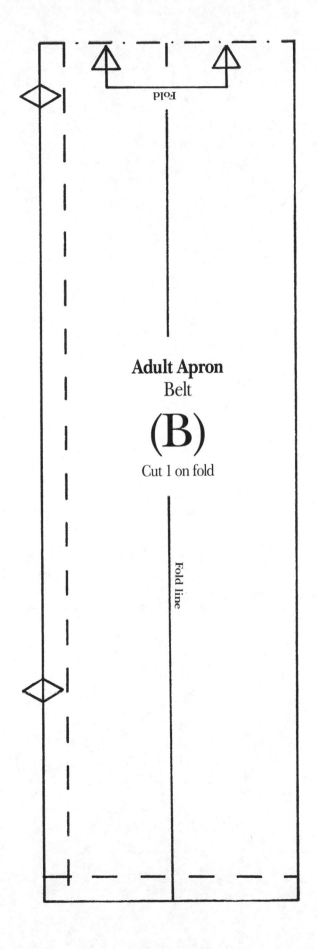

Fold

Adult Apron
Belt

(B)

Cut 1 on fold

Fold line

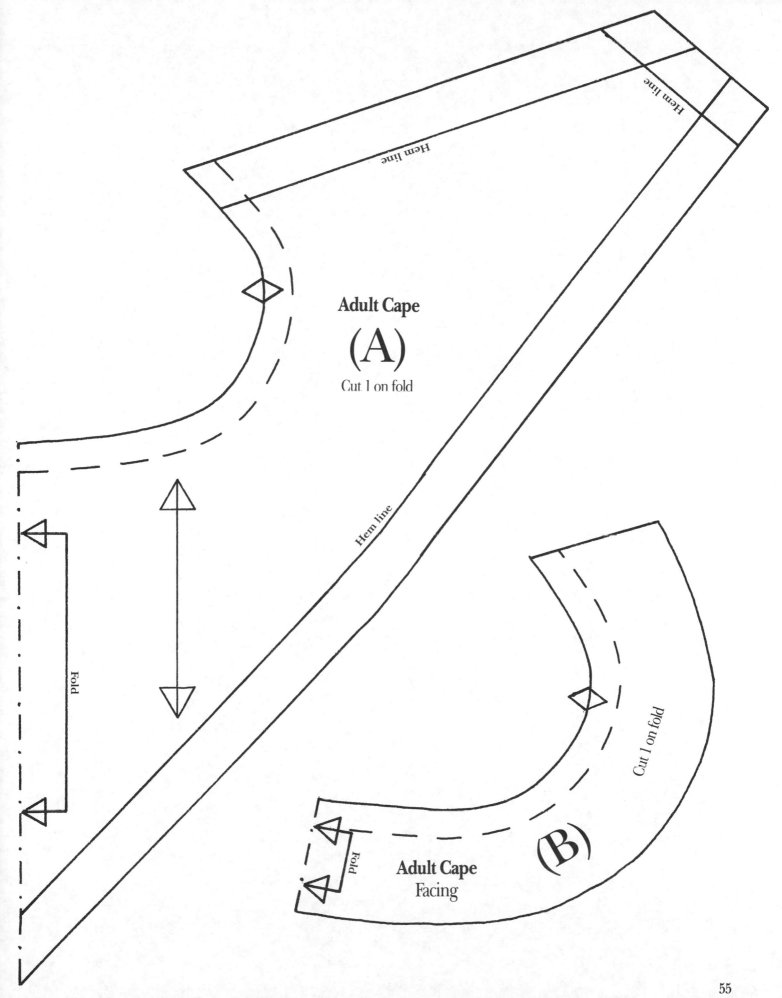

Adult Cape

(A)

Cut 1 on fold

Hem line

Hem line

Hem line

Fold

Adult Cape
Facing

Fold

Cut 1 on fold

(B)

55

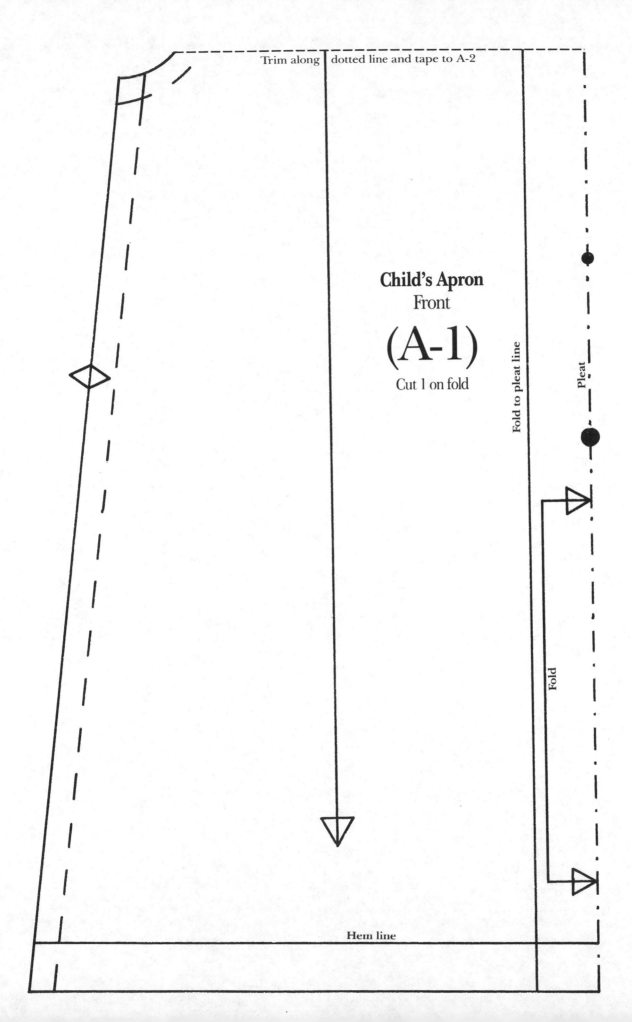

Trim along dotted line and tape to A-2

Child's Apron
Front

(A-1)

Cut 1 on fold

Fold to pleat line

Pleat

Fold

Hem line

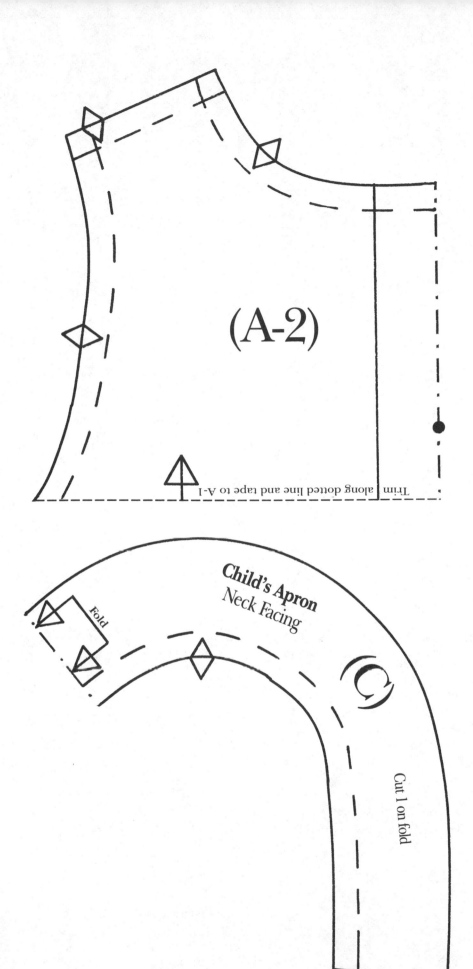

(A-2)

Trim along dotted line and tape to A-1

Child's Apron
Neck Facing

(C)

Fold

Cut 1 on fold

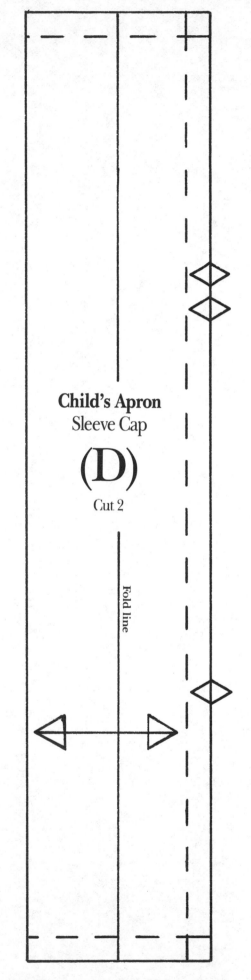

Child's Apron
Sleeve Cap

(D)

Cut 2

Fold line

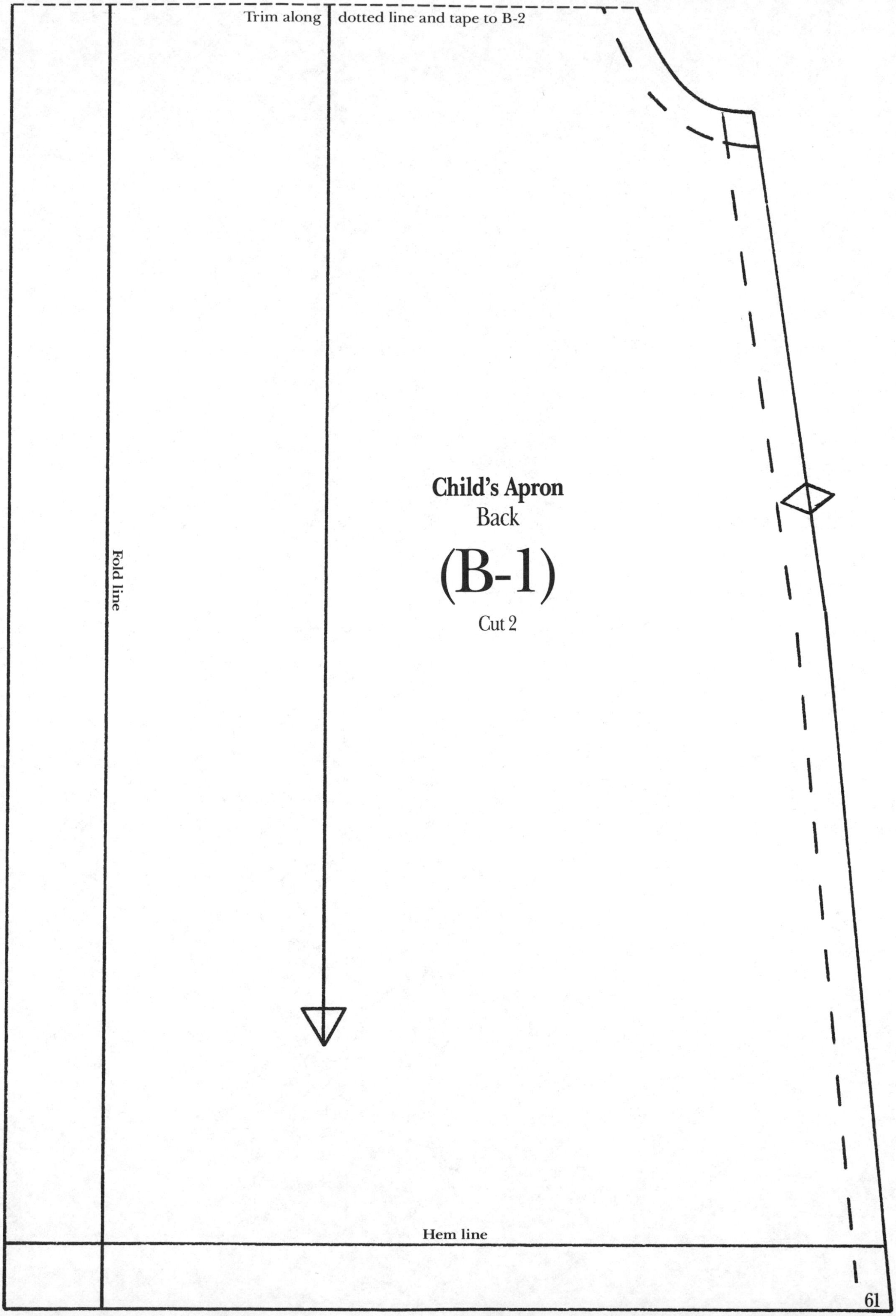

Trim along | dotted line and tape to B-2

Fold line

Child's Apron
Back

(B-1)

Cut 2

Hem line

61

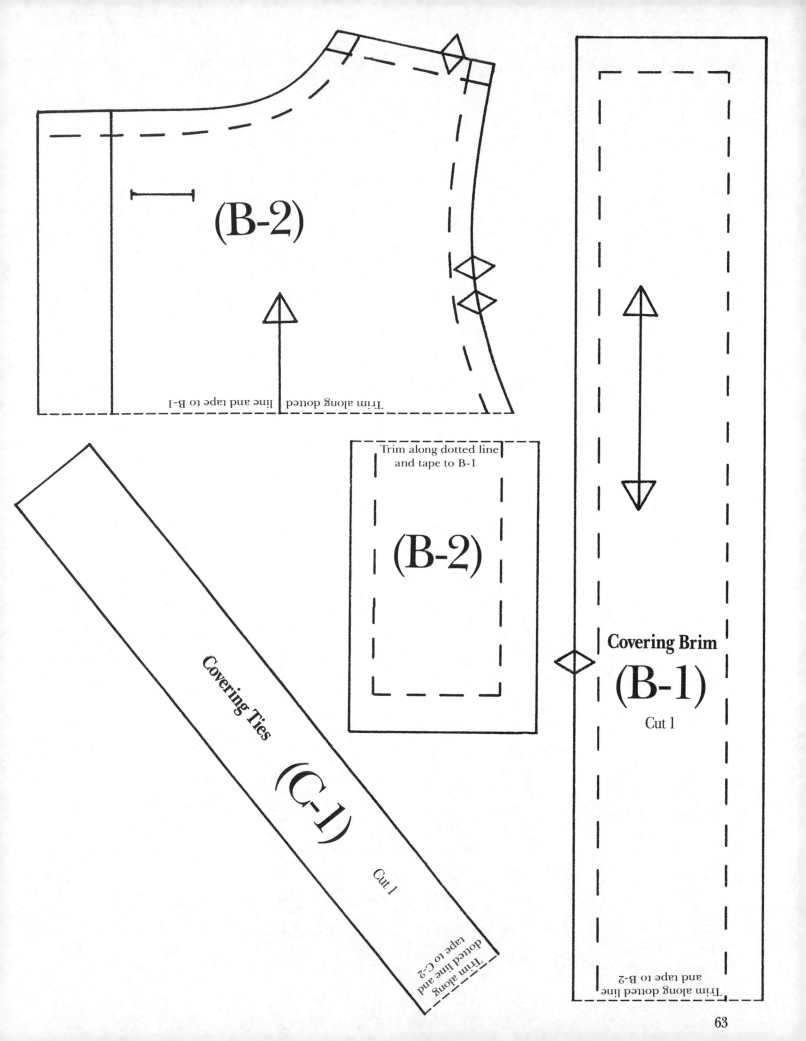

(B-2)

Trim along dotted line and tape to B-1

Trim along dotted line
and tape to B-1

(B-2)

Covering Ties

(C-1)

Cut 1

Trim along
dotted line and
tape to C-2

Covering Brim

(B-1)

Cut 1

Trim along dotted line
and tape to B-2

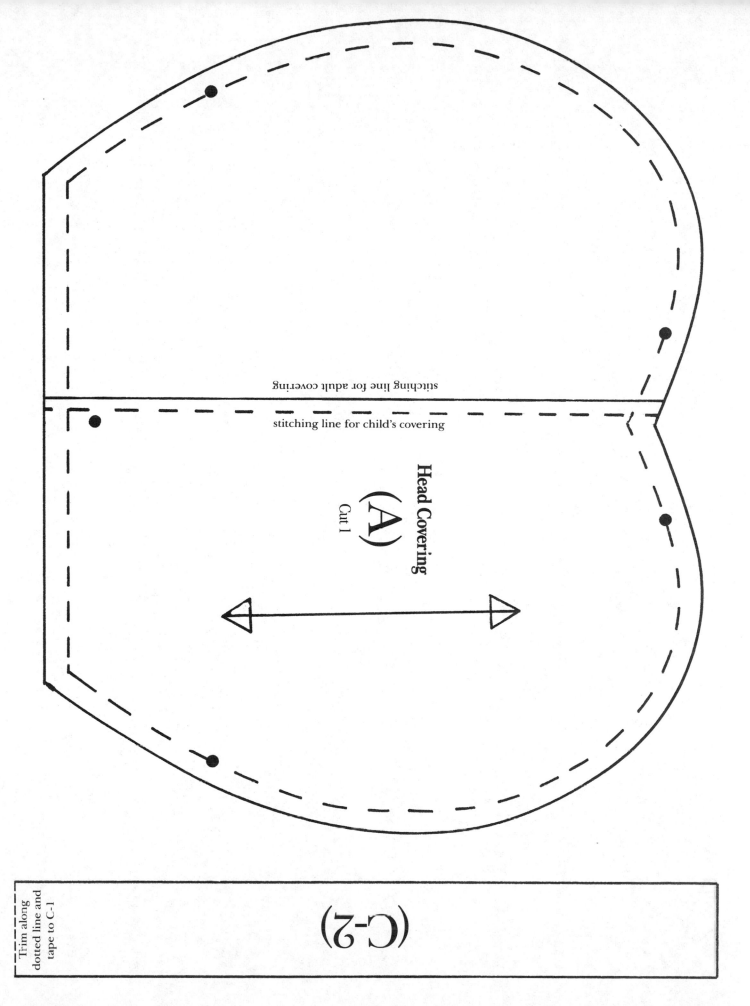

stitching line for adult covering

stitching line for child's covering

Head Covering

(A)
Cut 1

Trim along
dotted line and
tape to C-1

(C-2)

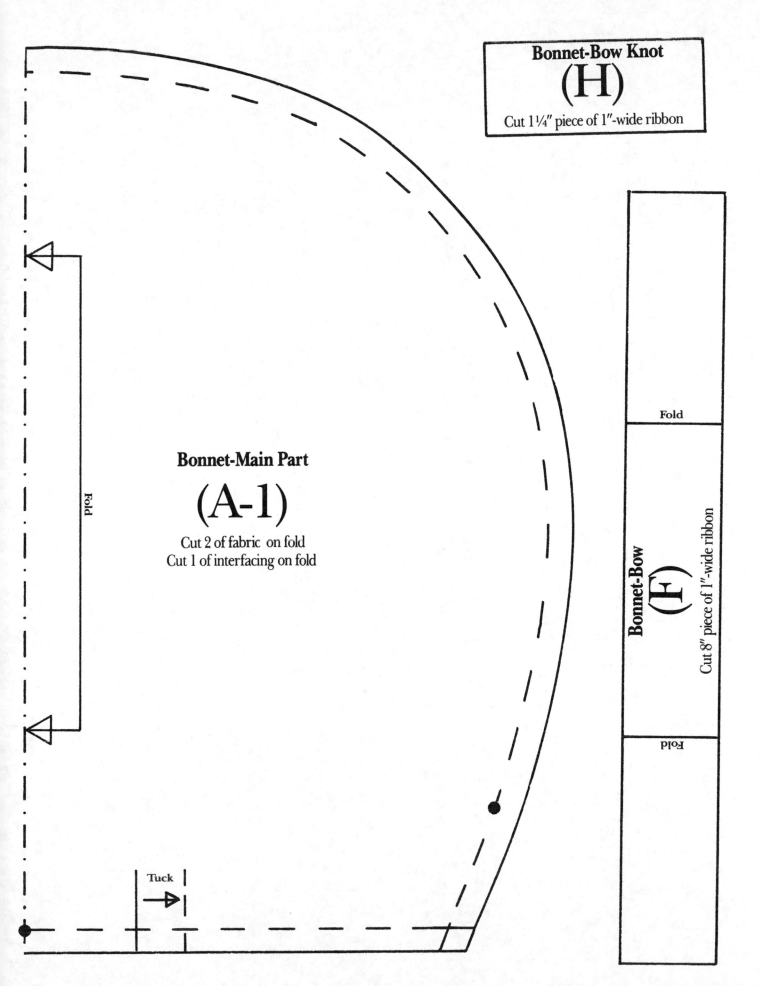

Bonnet-Bow Knot

(H)

Cut 1¼″ piece of 1″-wide ribbon

Bonnet-Main Part

(A-1)

Cut 2 of fabric on fold
Cut 1 of interfacing on fold

Fold

Fold

Tuck

Bonnet-Bow

(F)

Cut 8″ piece of 1″-wide ribbon

Fold

Fold

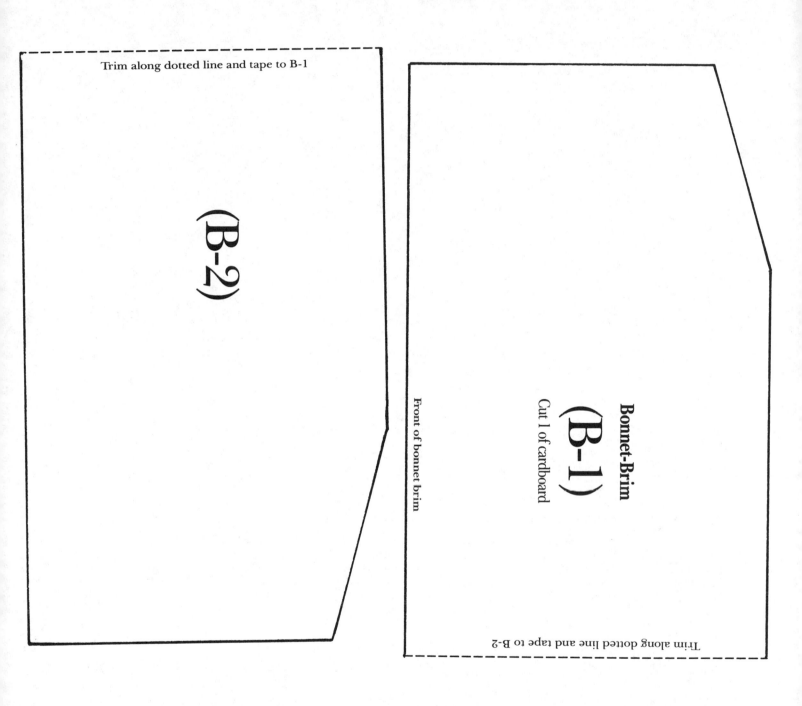

Trim along dotted line and tape to B-1

(B-2)

Bonnet-Brim

(B-1)

Cut 1 of cardboard

Front of bonnet brim

Trim along dotted line and tape to B-2

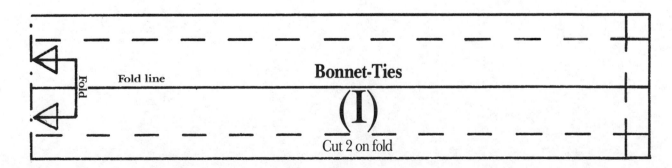

Bonnet-Ties

Fold line

Fold

(I)

Cut 2 on fold

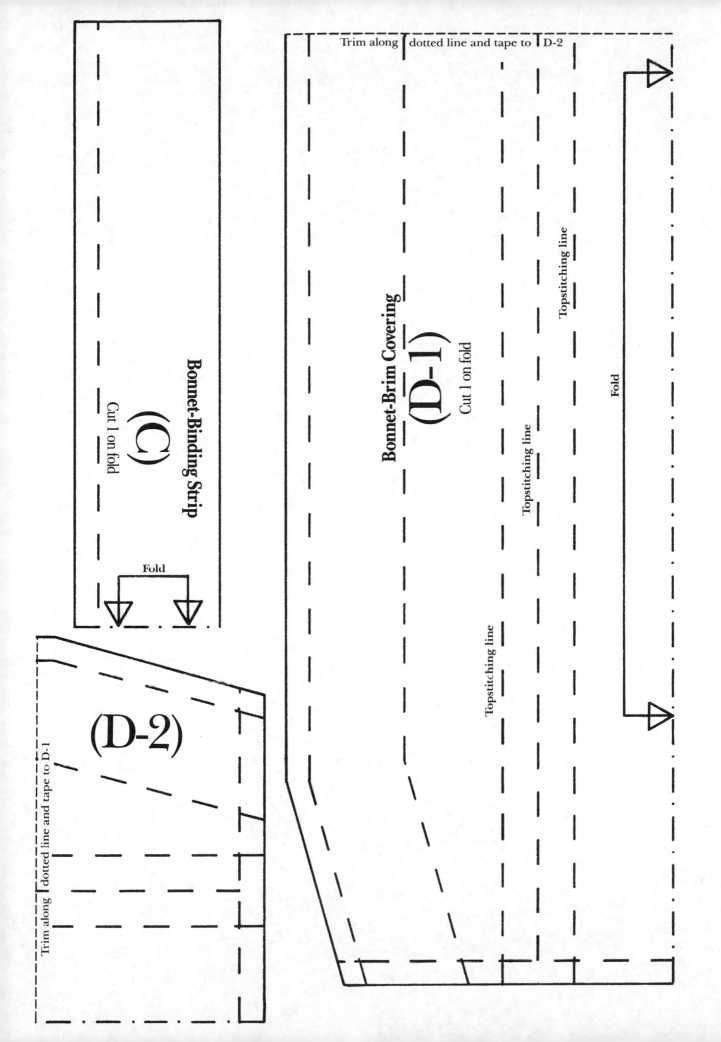

Trim along dotted line and tape to D-2

Bonnet-Brim Covering

(D-1)

Cut 1 on fold

Topstitching line

Topstitching line

Topstitching line

Topstitching line

Fold

Bonnet-Binding Strip

(C)

Cut 1 on fold

Fold

(D-2)

Trim along dotted line and tape to D-1

Trim along dotted line and tape to D-2

71

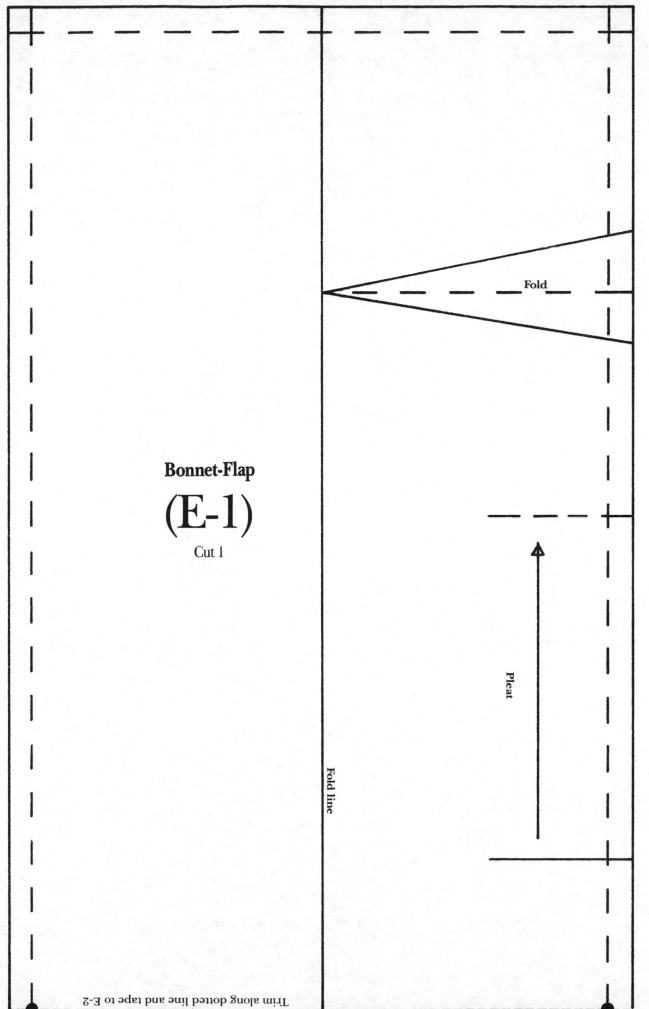

Bonnet-Flap

(E-1)

Cut 1

Fold

Fold line

Pleat

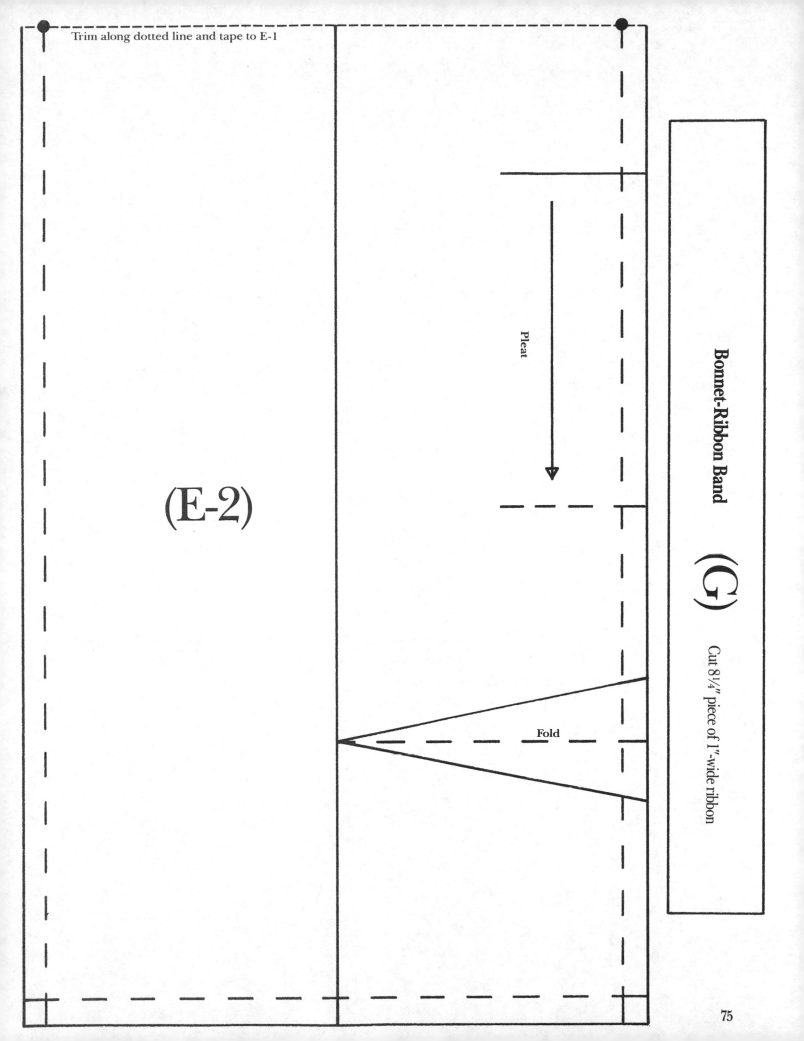

Trim along dotted line and tape to E-1

(E-2)

Pleat

Fold

Bonnet-Ribbon Band

(G)

Cut 8¼" piece of 1"-wide ribbon

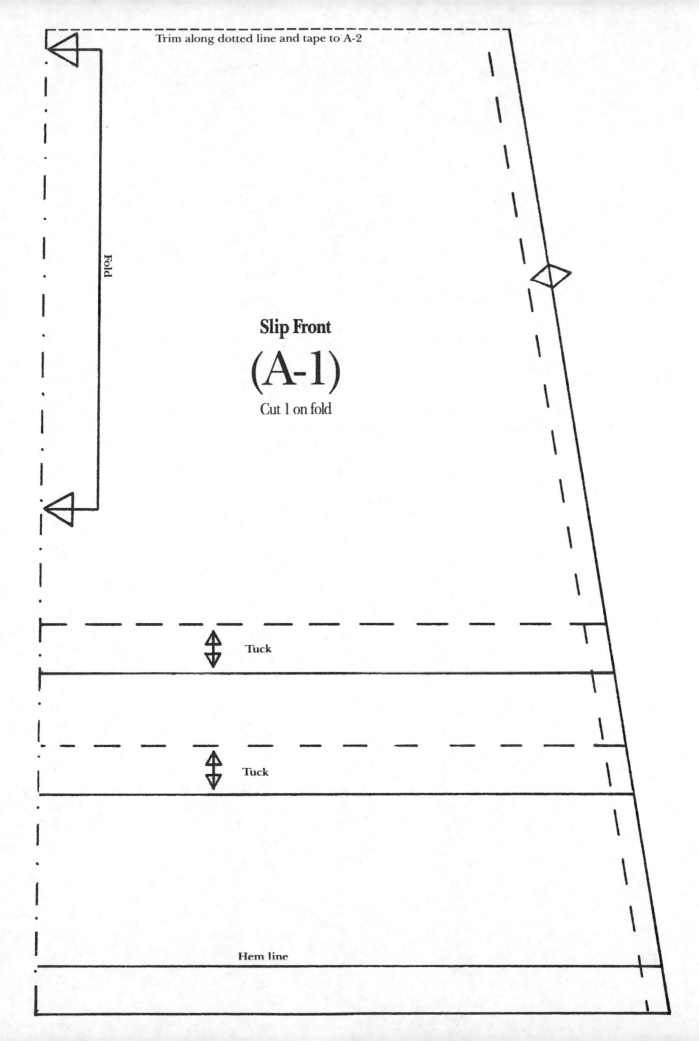

Trim along dotted line and tape to A-2

Fold

Slip Front

(A-1)

Cut 1 on fold

Tuck

Tuck

Hem line

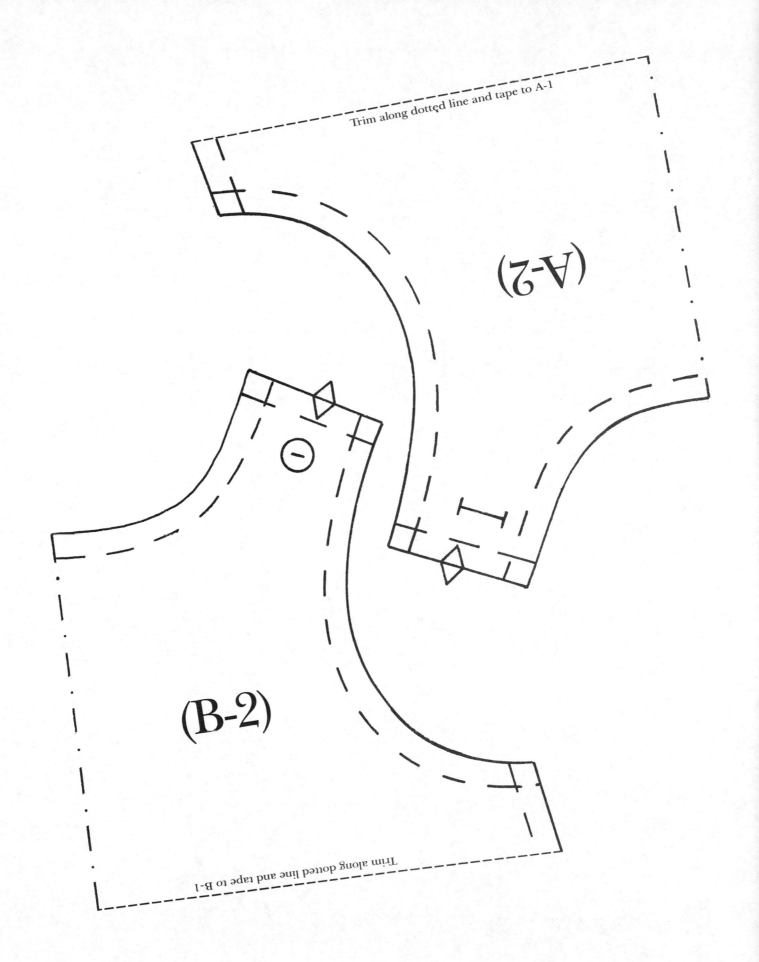

Trim along dotted line and tape to A-1

(A-2)

(B-2)

Trim along dotted line and tape to B-1

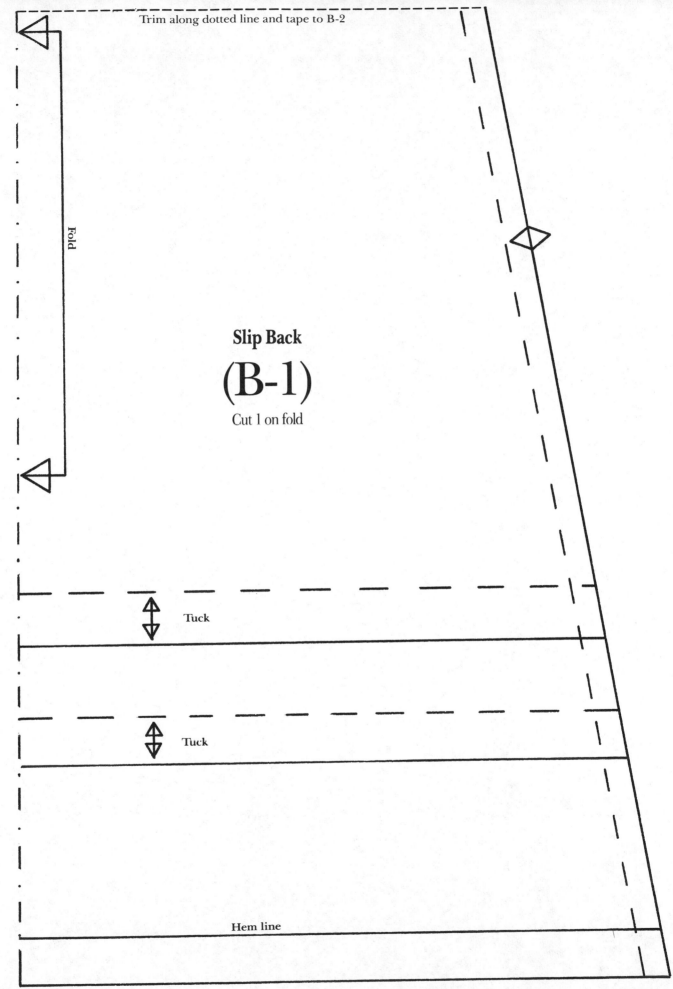

Trim along dotted line and tape to B-2

Fold

Slip Back

(B-1)

Cut 1 on fold

Tuck

Tuck

Hem line

81

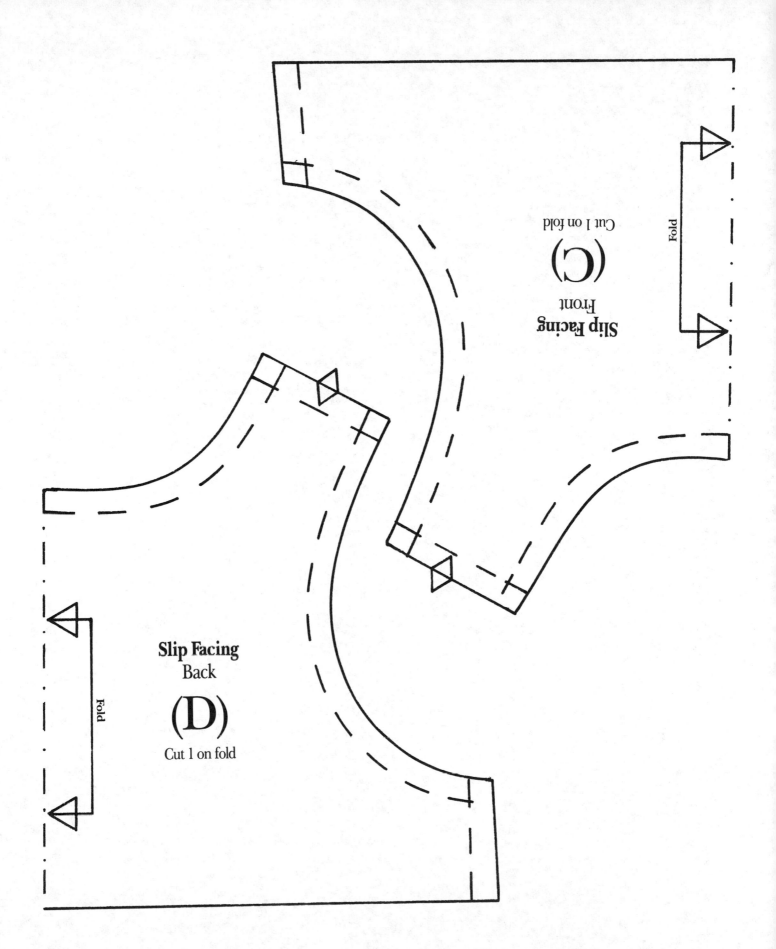

Slip Facing
Front

(C)

Cut 1 on fold

Fold

Slip Facing
Back

(D)

Cut 1 on fold

Fold

83

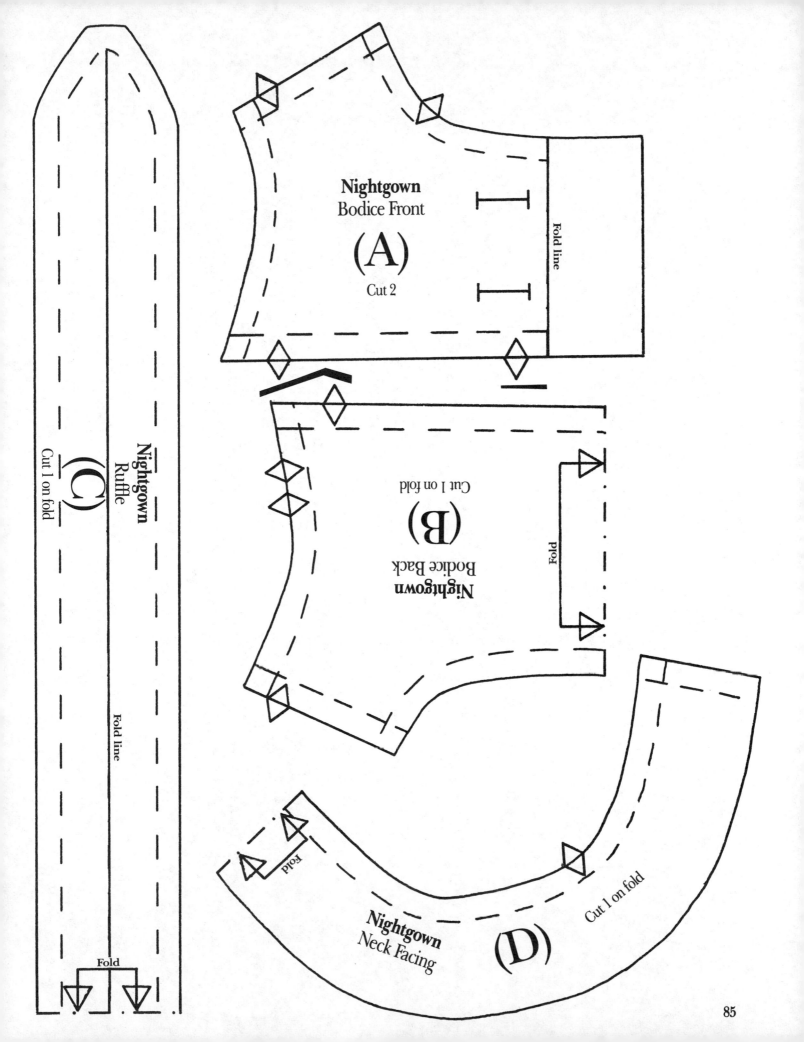

Nightgown
Bodice Front

(A)

Cut 2

Fold line

Nightgown
Ruffle

(C)

Cut 1 on fold

Fold line

Fold

Cut 1 on fold

Nightgown
Bodice Back

(B)

Fold

Nightgown
Neck Facing

(D)

Cut 1 on fold

Fold

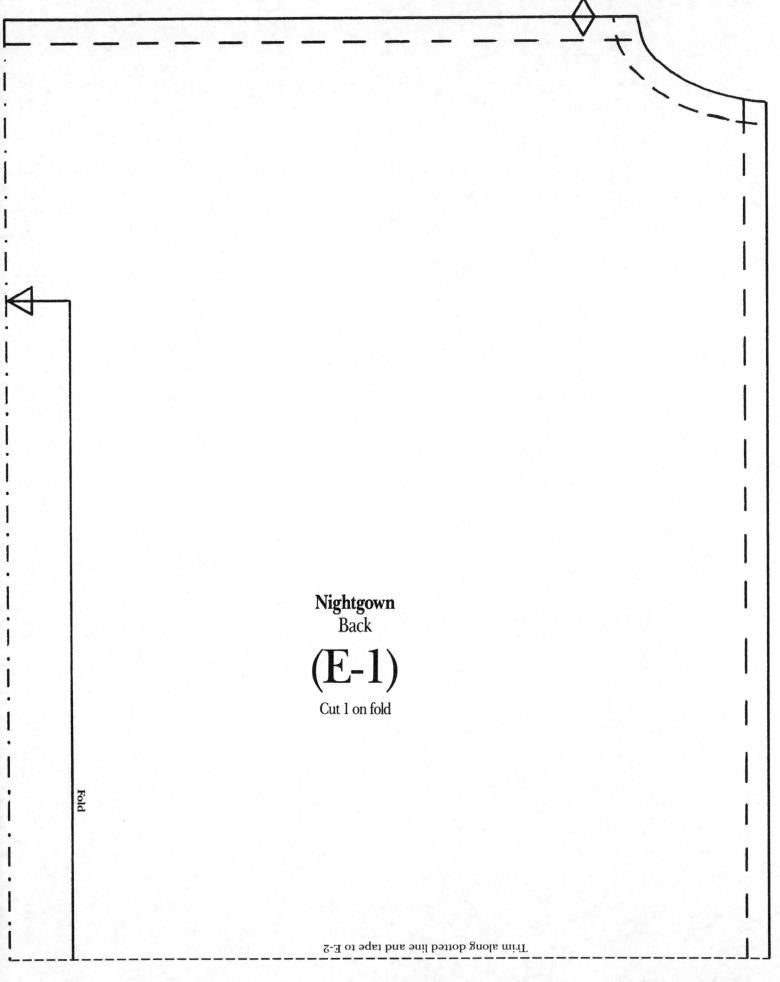

Nightgown
Back

(E-1)

Cut 1 on fold

Fold

Trim along dotted line and tape to E-2

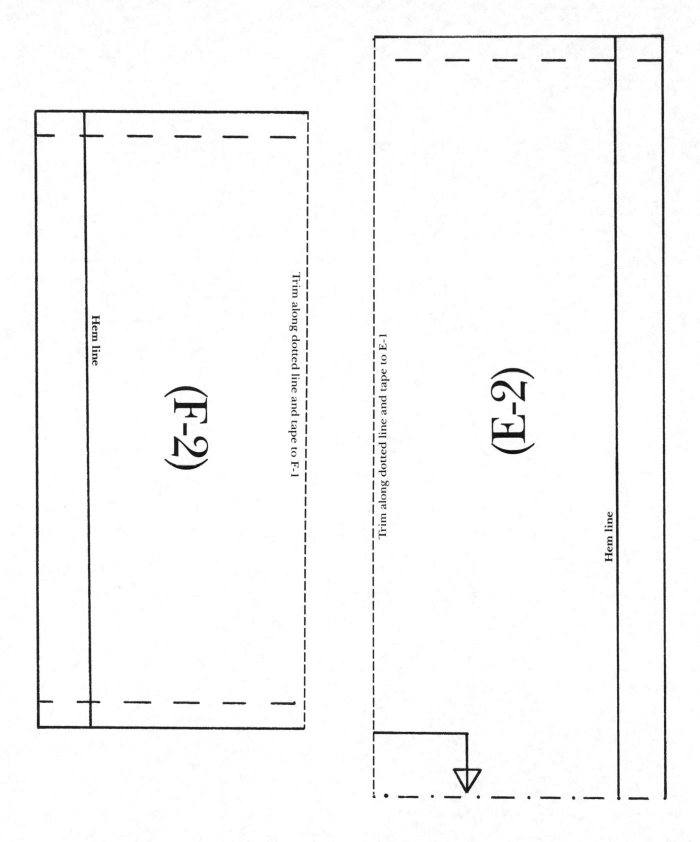

(F-2)

Hem line

Trim along dotted line and tape to F-1

(E-2)

Trim along dotted line and tape to E-1

Hem line

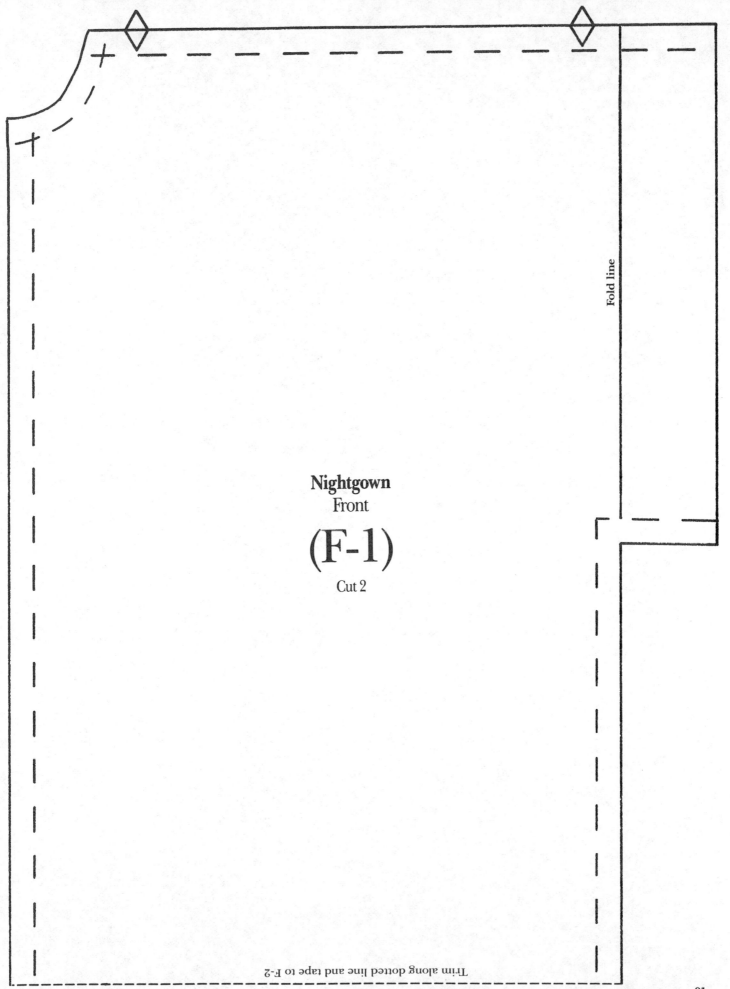

Nightgown
Front

(F-1)

Cut 2

Fold line

Trim along dotted line and tape to F-2

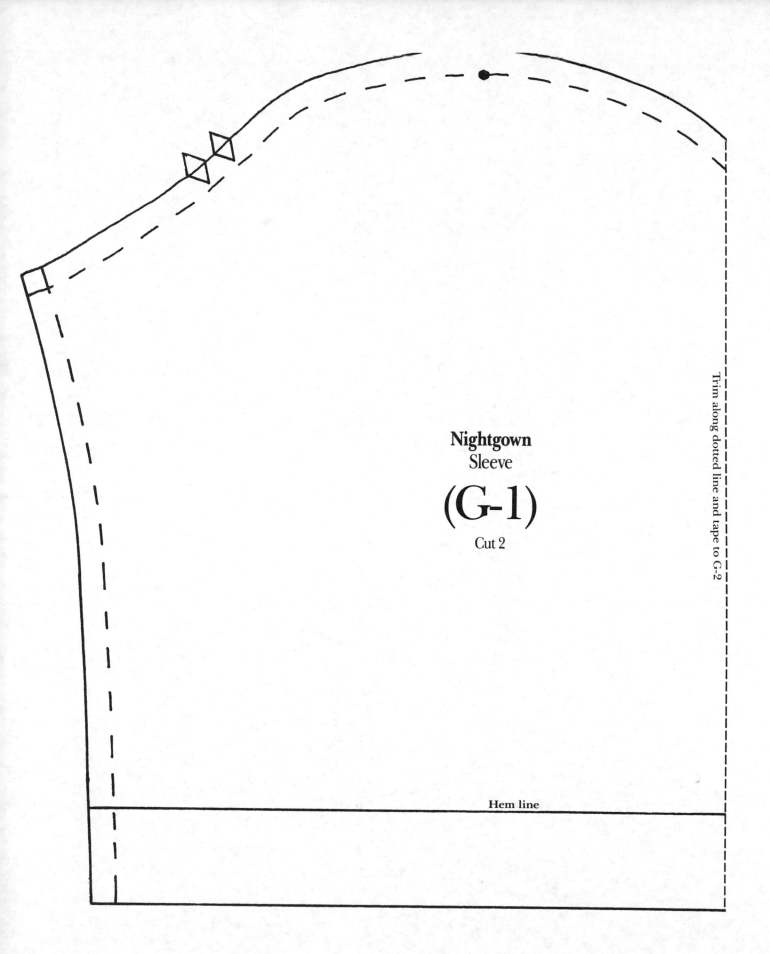

Nightgown
Sleeve

(G-1)

Cut 2

Hem line

Trim along dotted line and tape to G-2

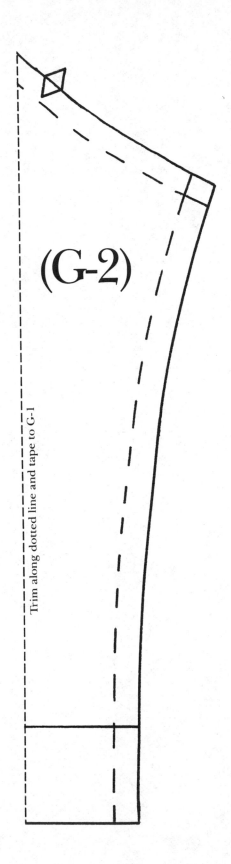

(G-2)

Trim along dotted line and tape to G-1

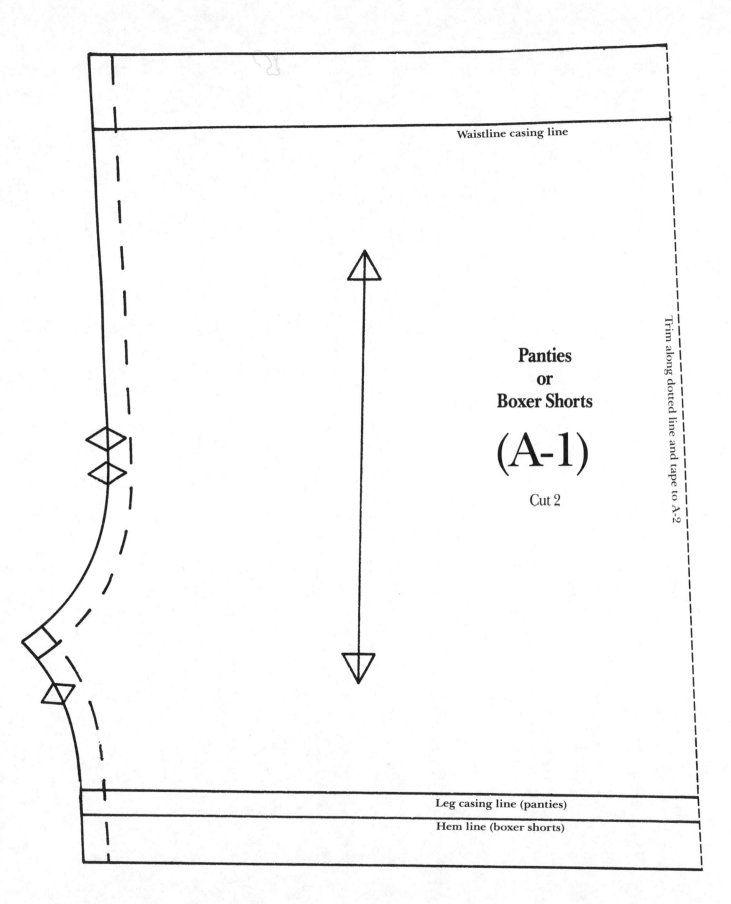

Waistline casing line

Trim along dotted line and tape to A-2

Panties
or
Boxer Shorts

(A-1)

Cut 2

Leg casing line (panties)

Hem line (boxer shorts)

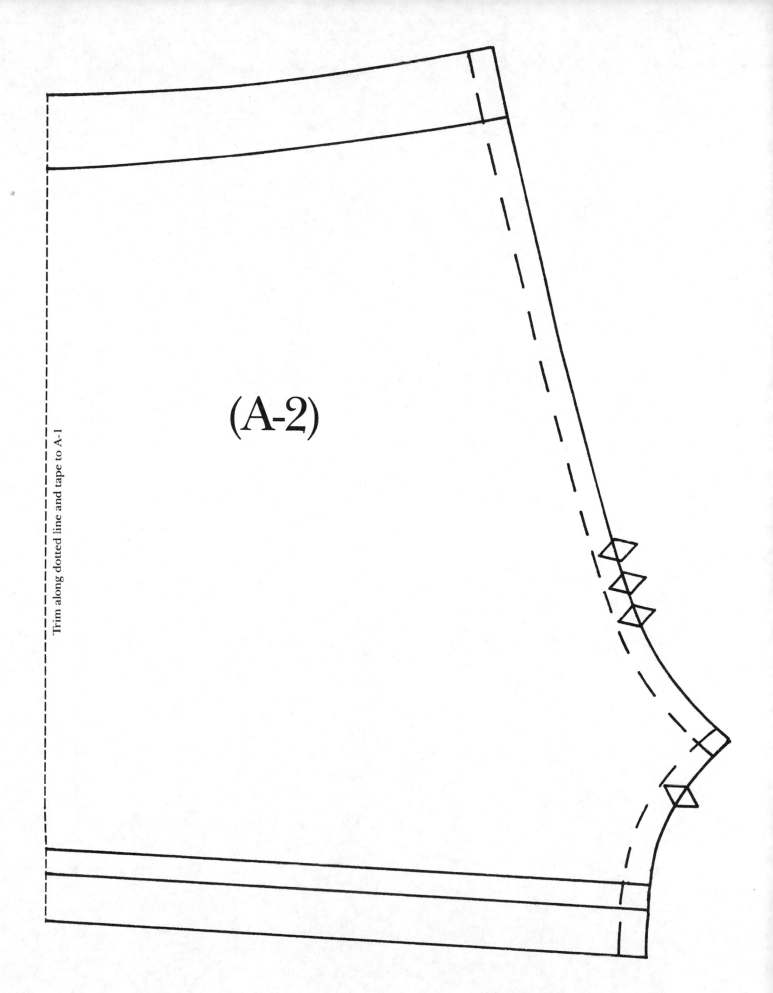

(A-2)

Trim along dotted line and tape to A-1

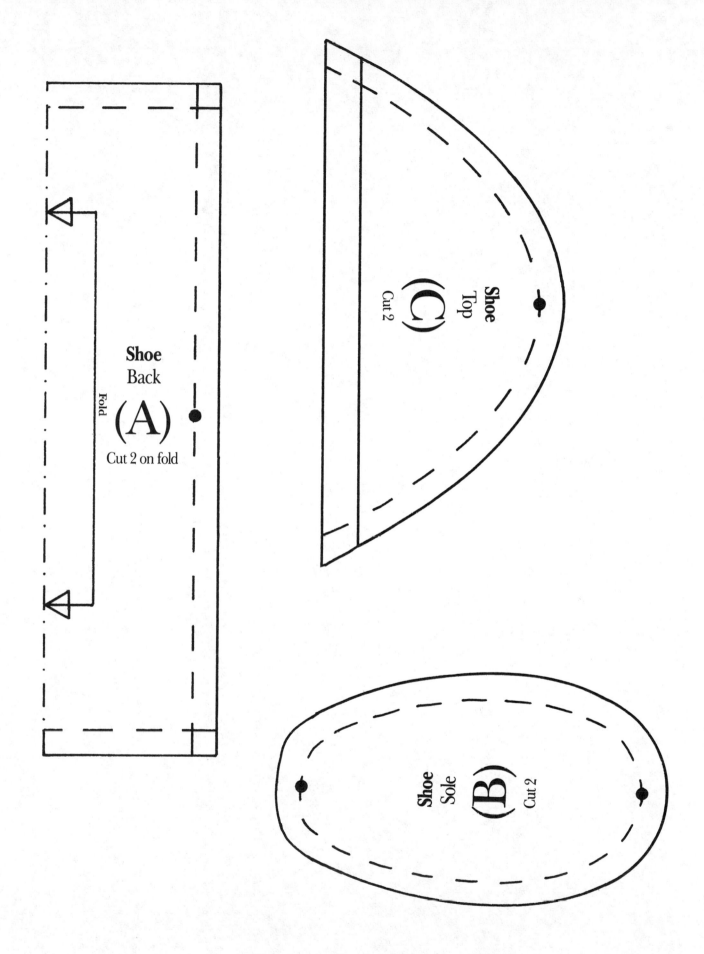

Shoe
Back
Fold
(A)
Cut 2 on fold

Shoe
Top
(C)
Cut 2

Shoe
Sole
(B)
Cut 2

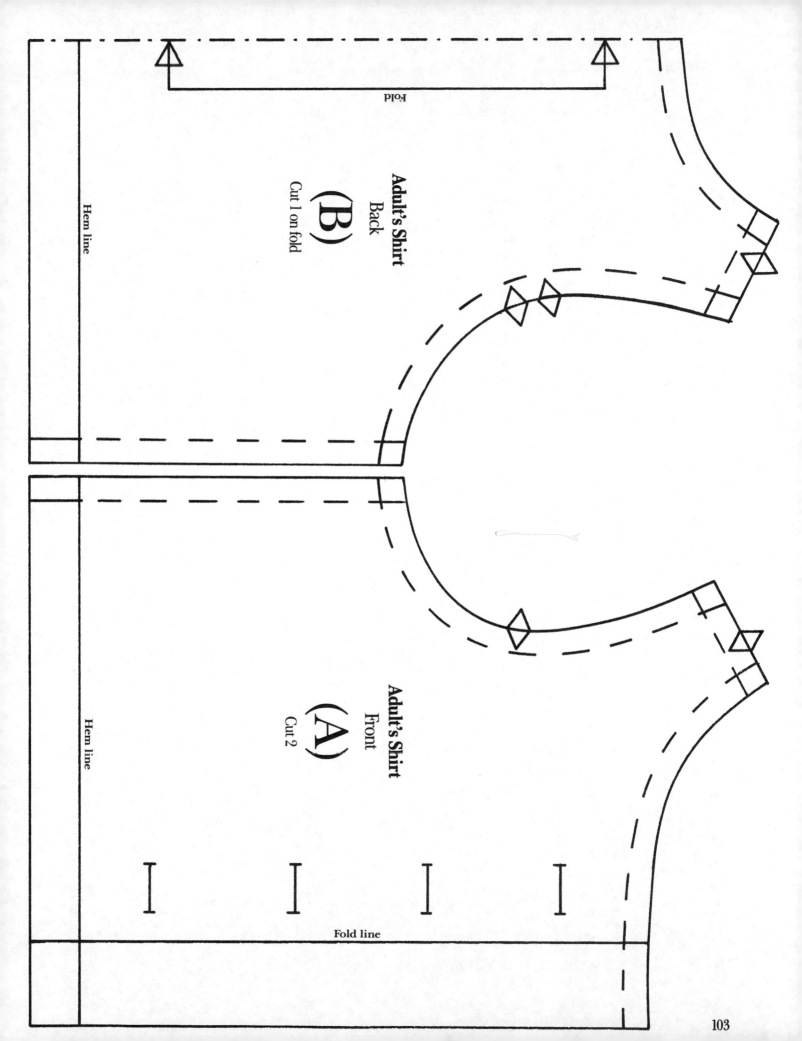

Fold

Adult's Shirt
Back

(B)
Cut 1 on fold

Hem line

Adult's Shirt
Front

(A)
Cut 2

Hem line

Fold line

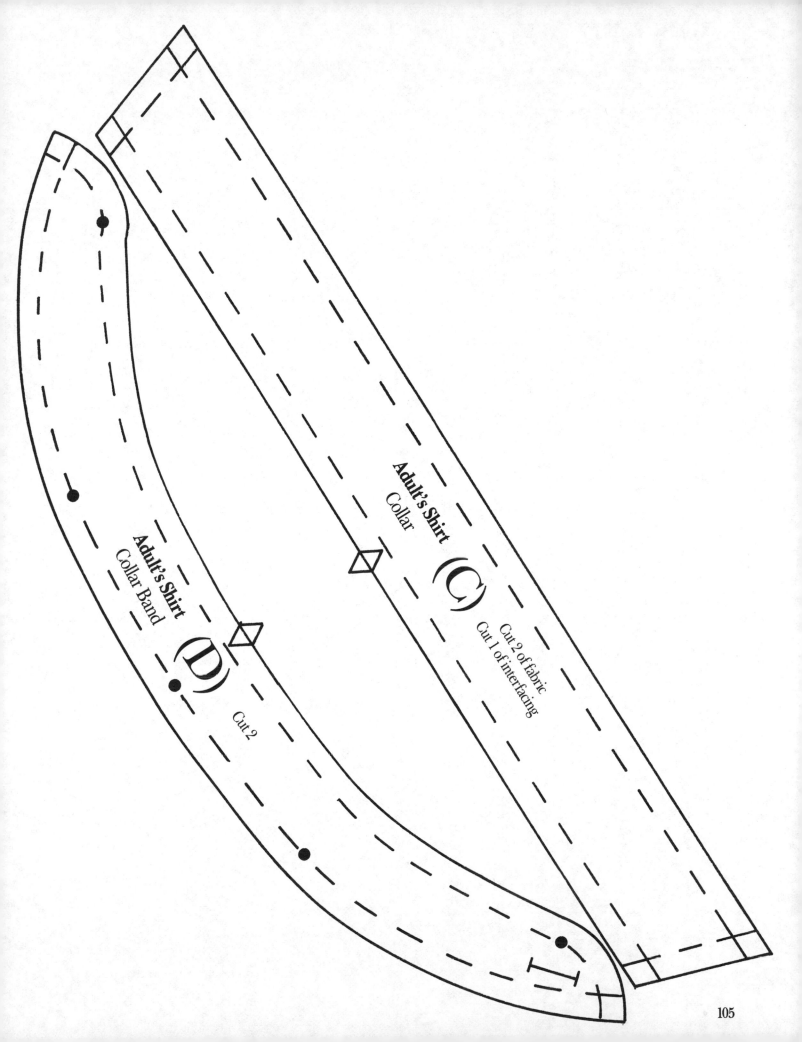

Adult's Shirt
Collar

(C)

Cut 2 of fabric
Cut 1 of interfacing

Adult's Shirt
Collar Band

(D)

Cut 2

105

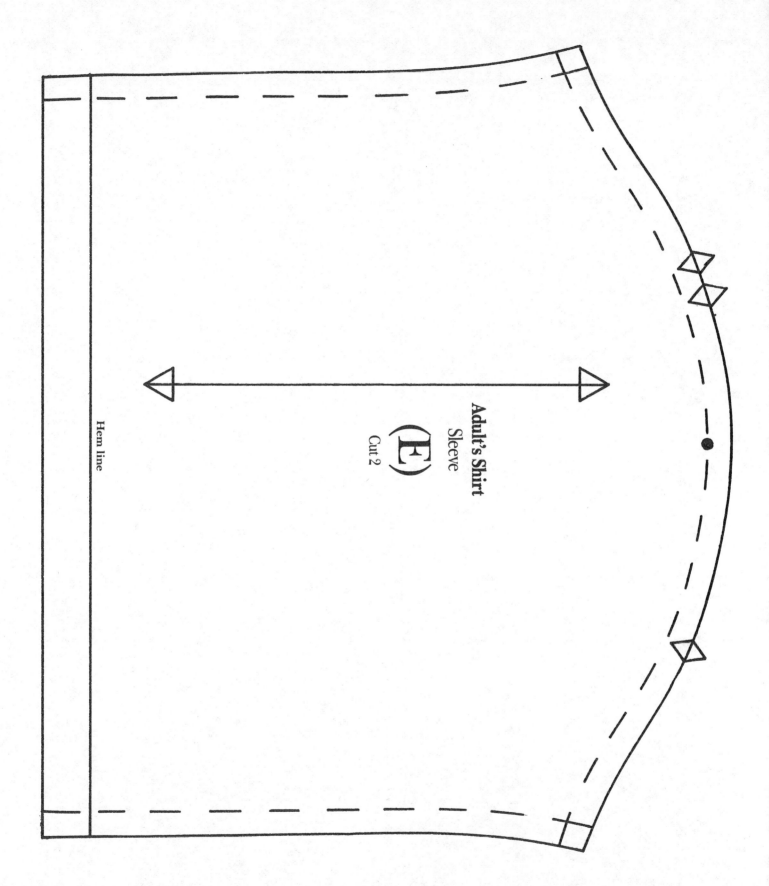

Hem line

Adult's Shirt
Sleeve
(E)
Cut 2

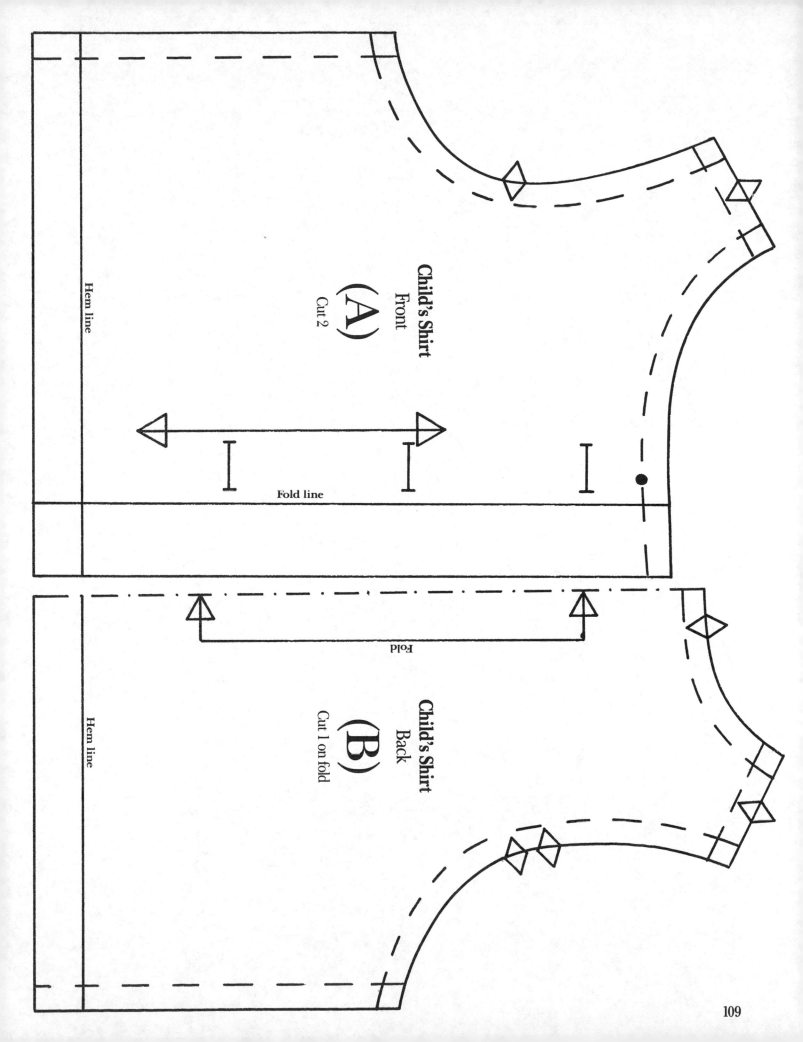

Hem line

Child's Shirt
Front
(A)
Cut 2

Fold line

Child's Shirt
Back
(B)
Cut 1 on fold

Fold

Hem line

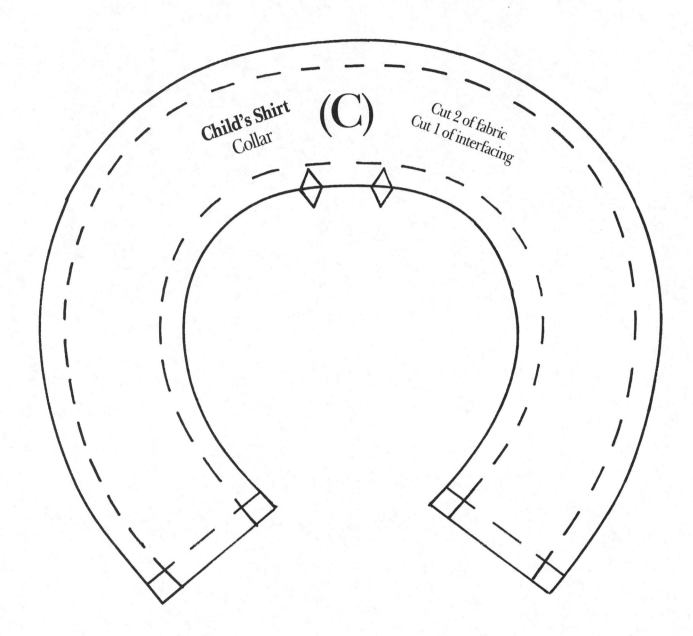

Child's Shirt (C)
Collar

Cut 2 of fabric
Cut 1 of interfacing

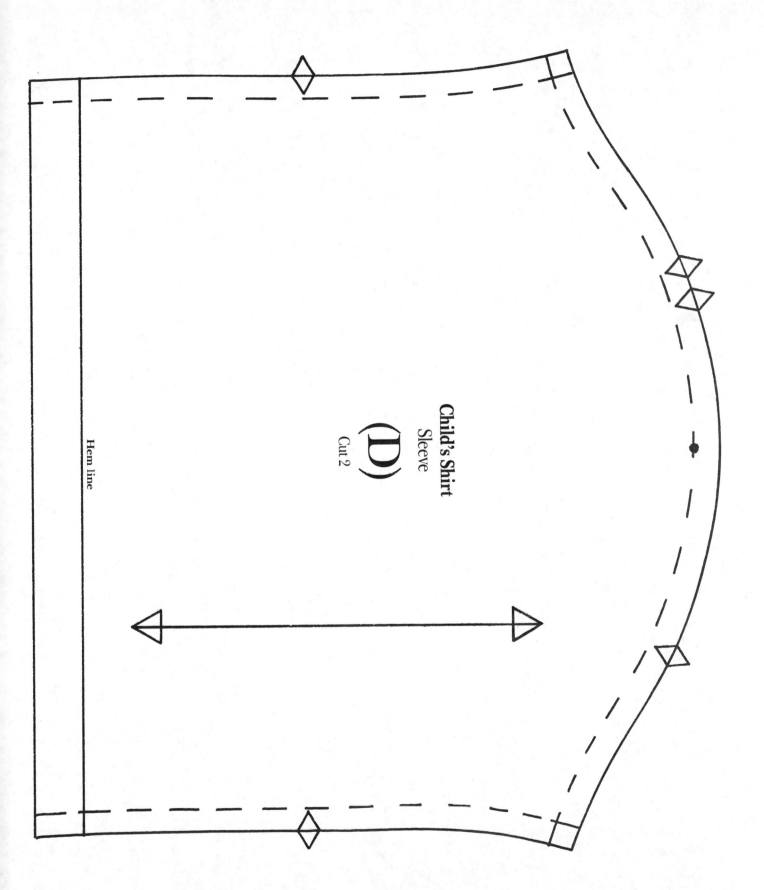

Child's Shirt
Sleeve
(D)
Cut 2

Hem line

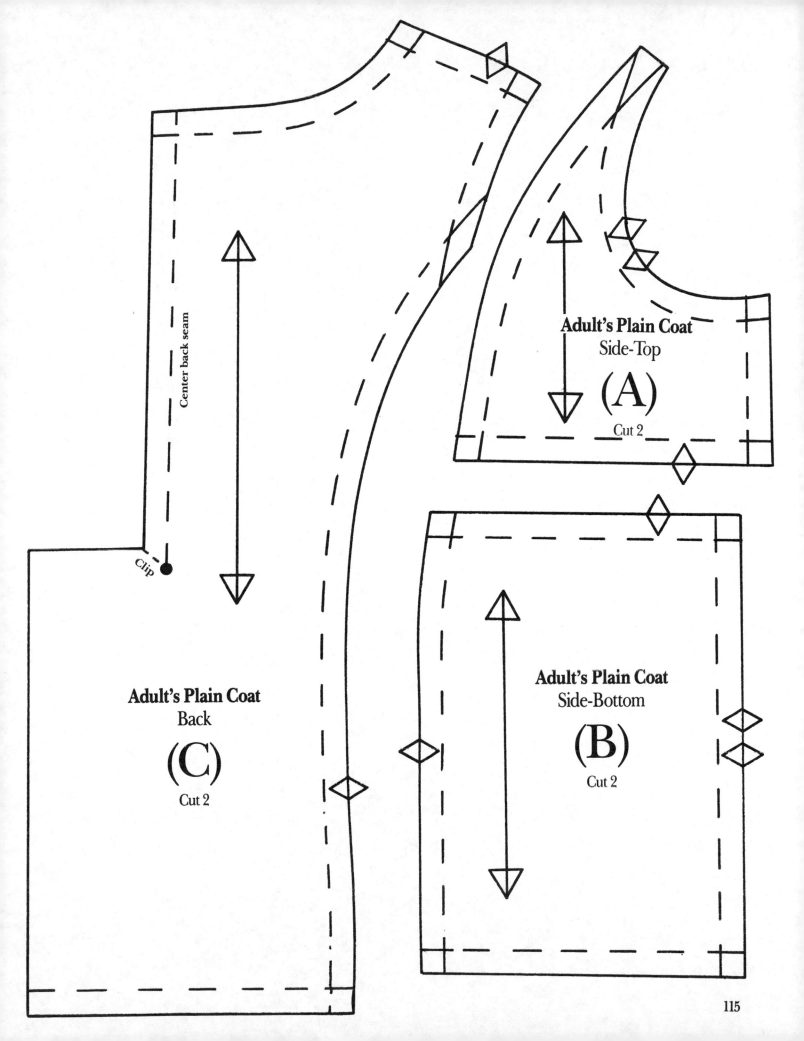

Adult's Plain Coat
Side-Top

(A)

Cut 2

Adult's Plain Coat
Side-Bottom

(B)

Cut 2

Center back seam

Clip

Adult's Plain Coat
Back

(C)

Cut 2

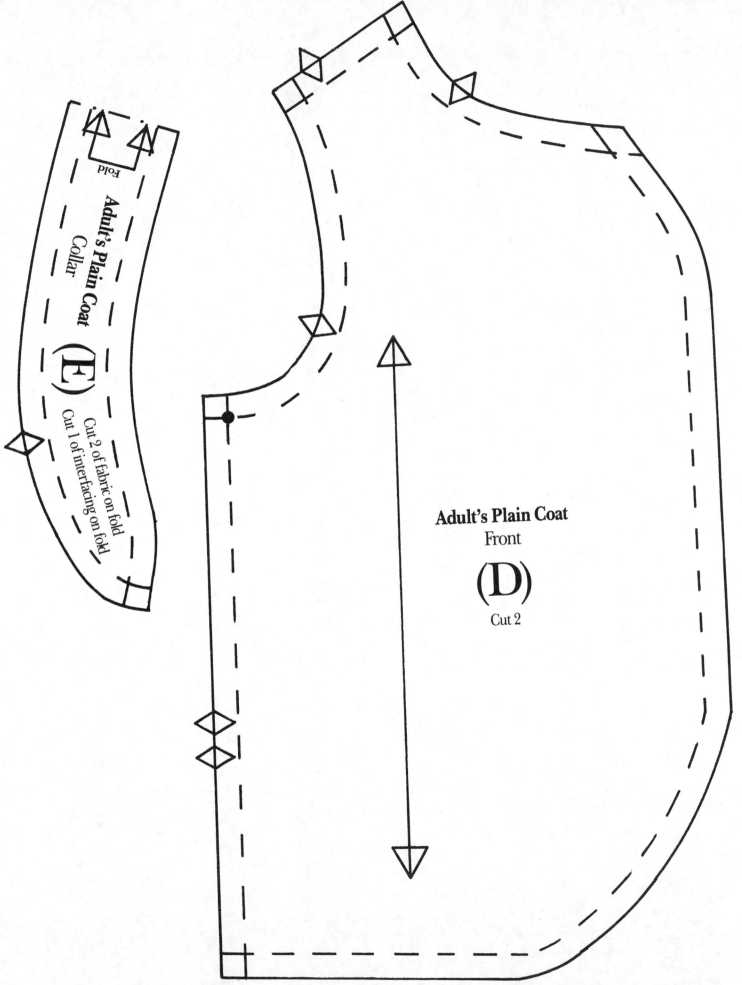

Adult's Plain Coat
Collar

(E)

Cut 2 of fabric on fold
Cut 1 of interfacing on fold

Fold

Adult's Plain Coat
Front

(D)

Cut 2

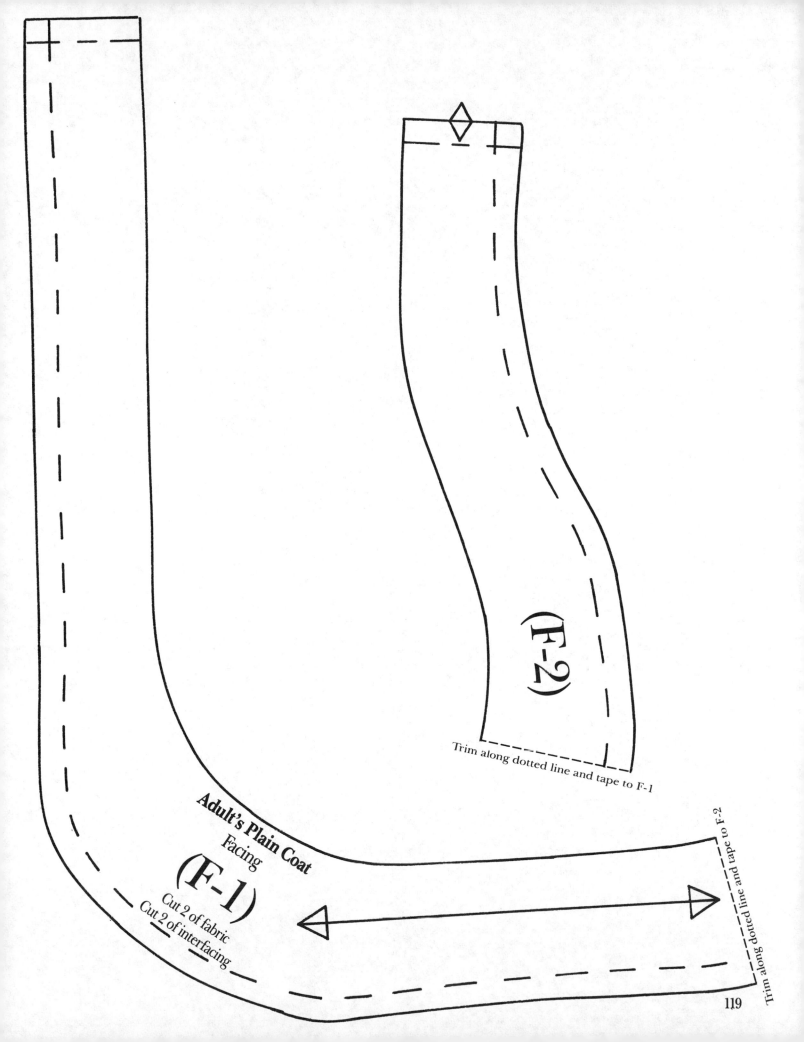

Adult's Plain Coat
Facing
(F-1)
Cut 2 of fabric
Cut 2 of interfacing

(F-2)

Trim along dotted line and tape to F-1

Trim along dotted line and tape to F-2

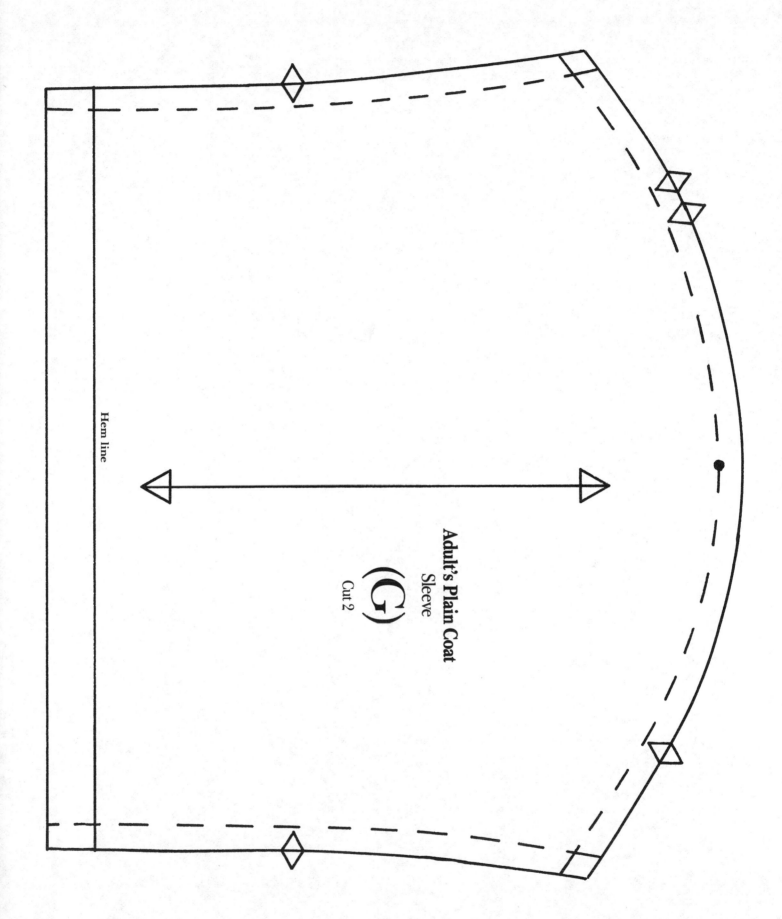

Hem line

Adult's Plain Coat
Sleeve

(G)
Cut 2

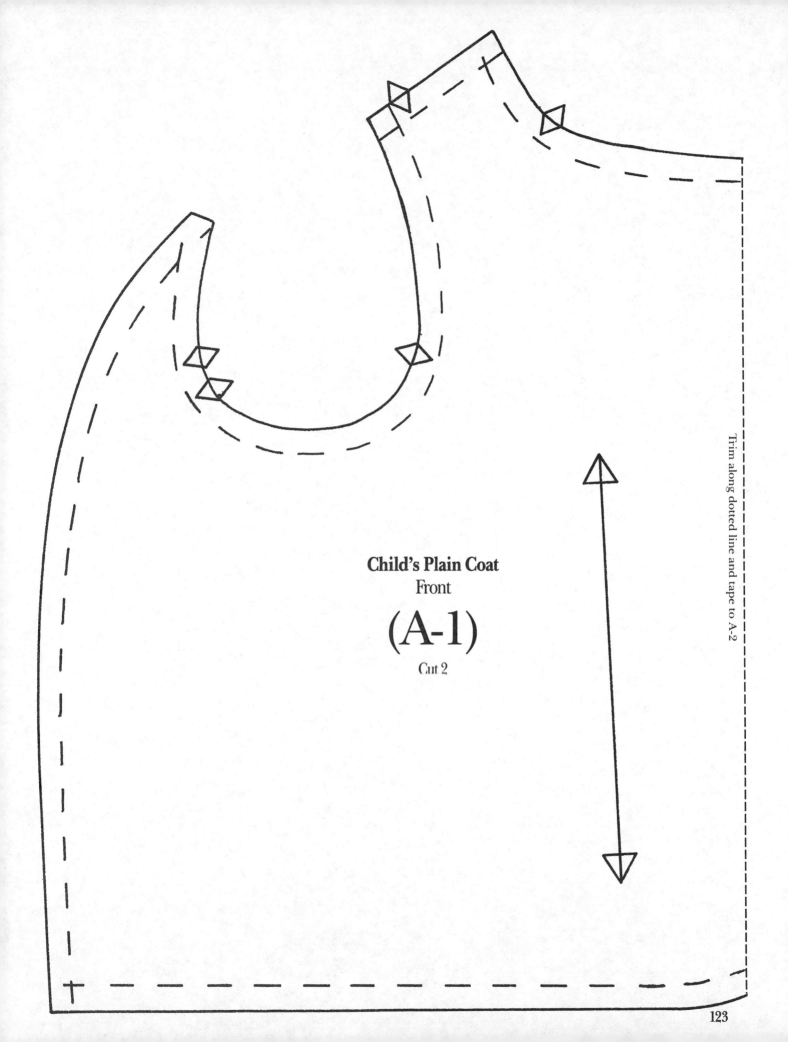

Child's Plain Coat
Front

(A-1)

Cut 2

Trim along dotted line and tape to A-2

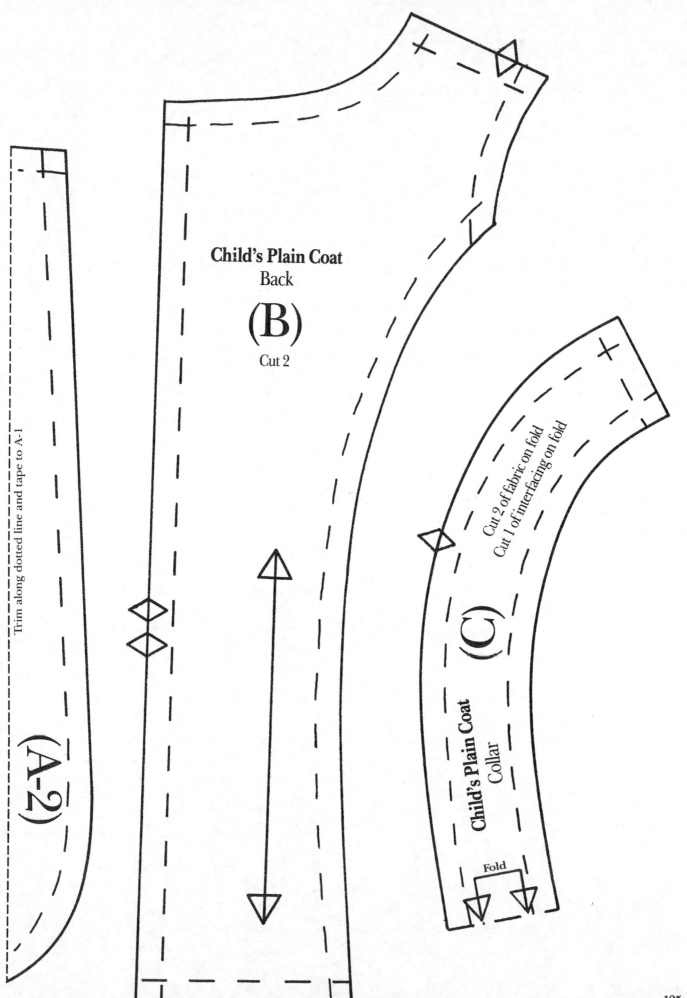

Trim along dotted line and tape to A-1

(A-2)

Child's Plain Coat
Back

(B)

Cut 2

Child's Plain Coat
Collar

(C)

Cut 2 of fabric on fold
Cut 1 of interfacing on fold

Fold

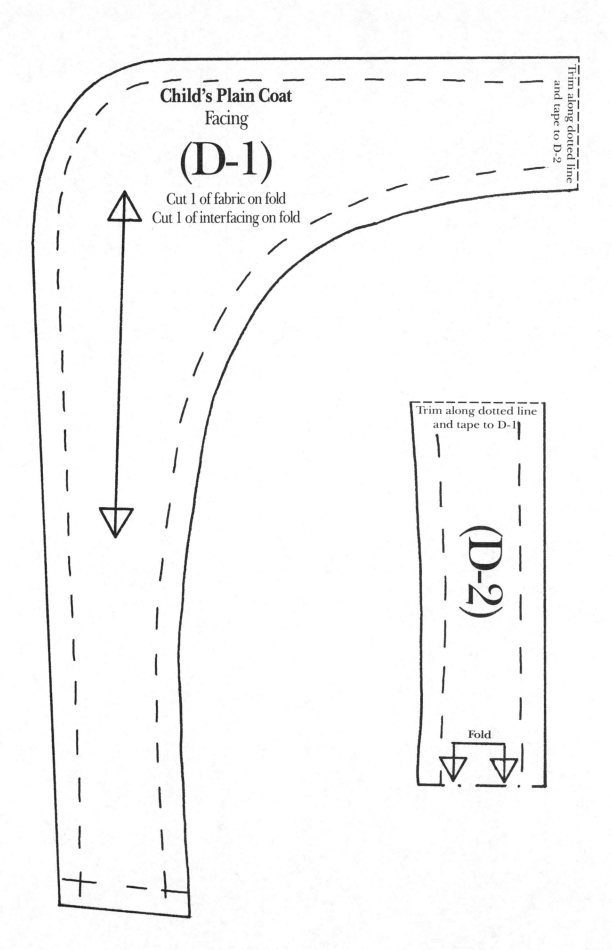

Child's Plain Coat
Facing

(D-1)

Cut 1 of fabric on fold
Cut 1 of interfacing on fold

Trim along dotted line
and tape to D-2

Trim along dotted line
and tape to D-1

(D-2)

Fold

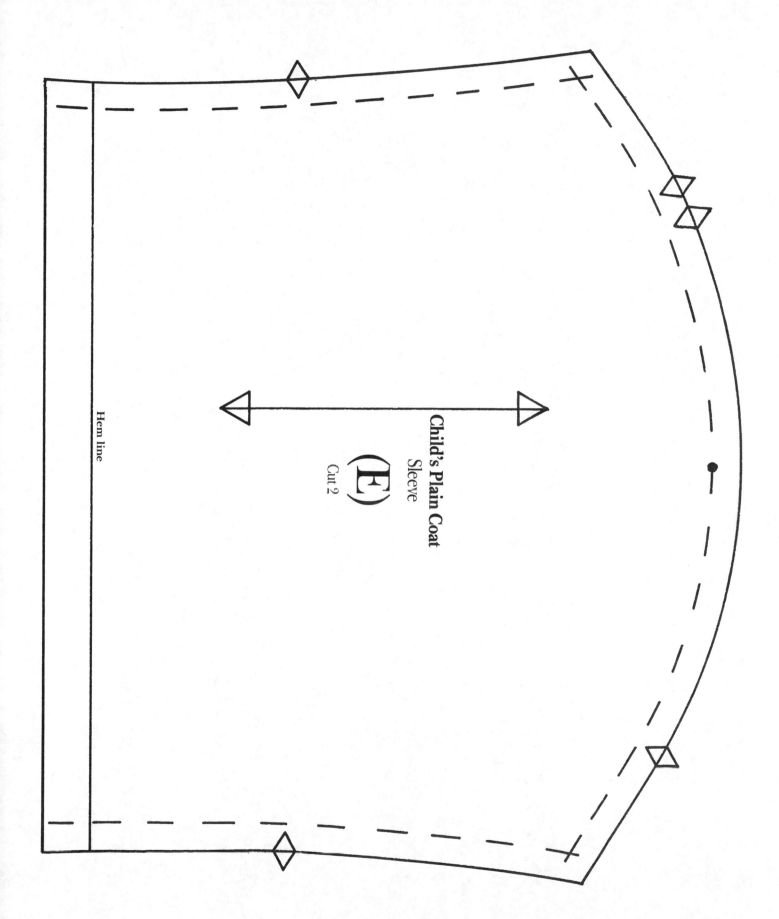

Hem line

Child's Plain Coat
Sleeve

(E)
Cut 2

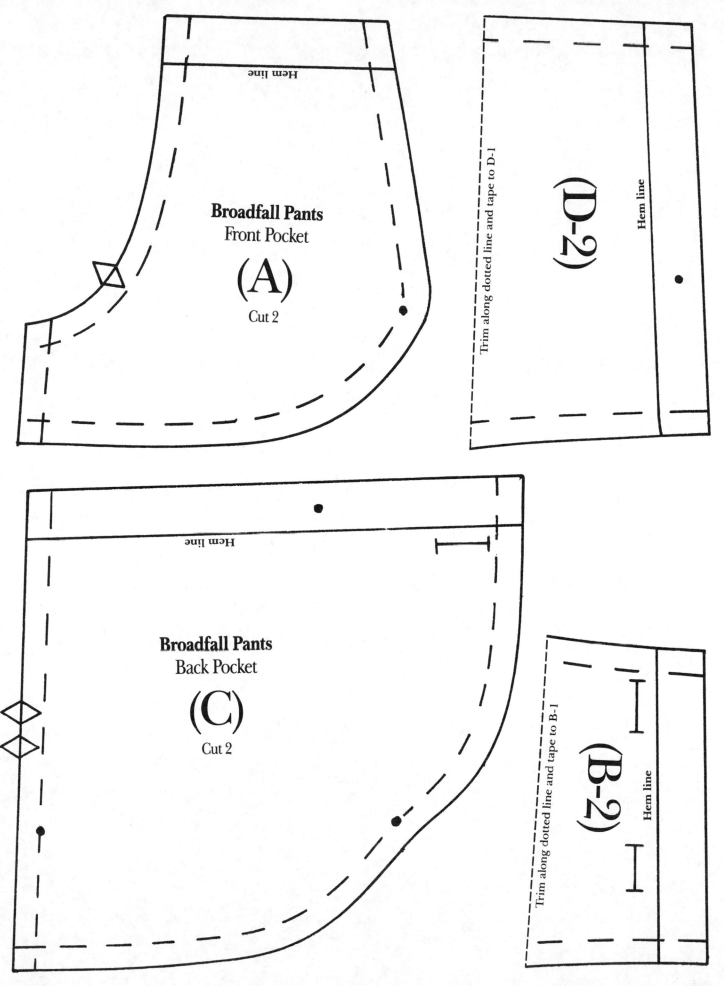

Broadfall Pants
Front Pocket

(A)

Cut 2

Hem line

(D-2)

Trim along dotted line and tape to D-1

Hem line

Broadfall Pants
Back Pocket

(C)

Cut 2

Hem line

(B-2)

Trim along dotted line and tape to B-1

Hem line

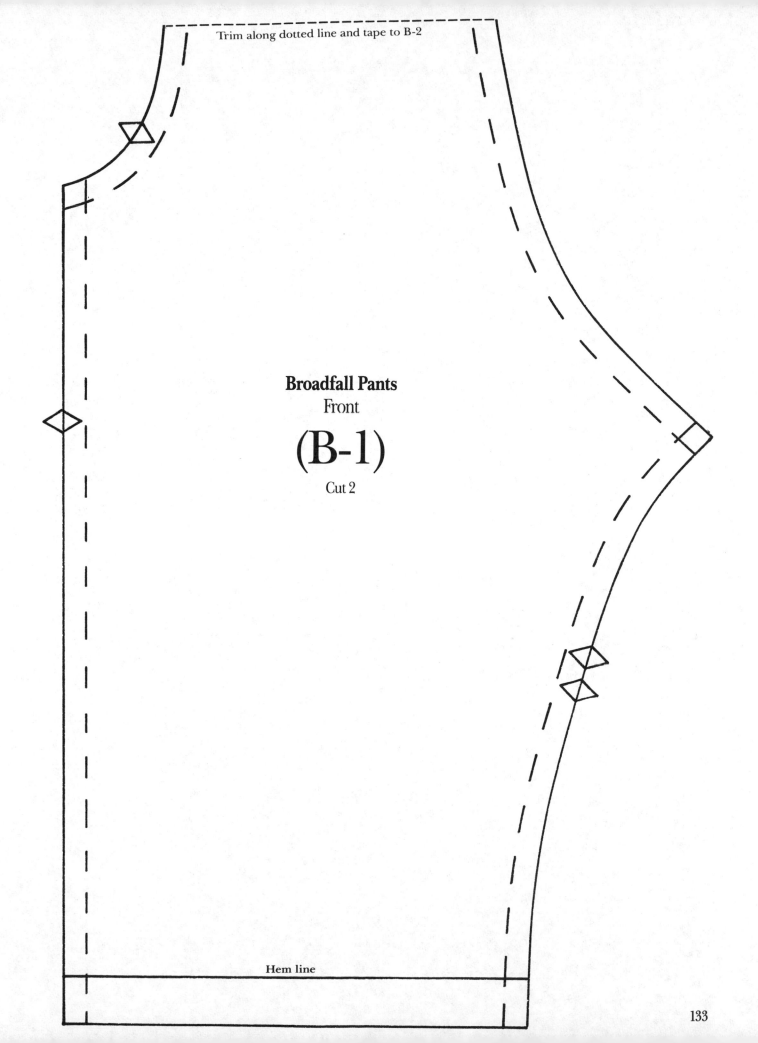

Trim along dotted line and tape to B-2

Broadfall Pants
Front

(B-1)

Cut 2

Hem line

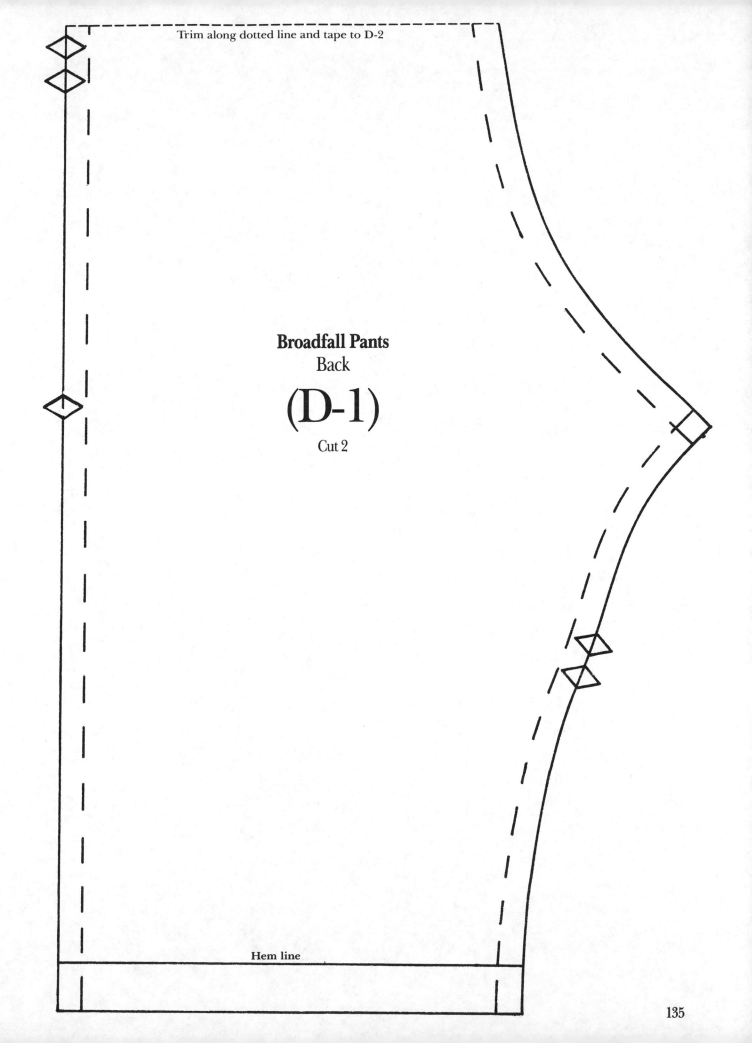

Trim along dotted line and tape to D-2

Broadfall Pants
Back
(D-1)
Cut 2

Hem line

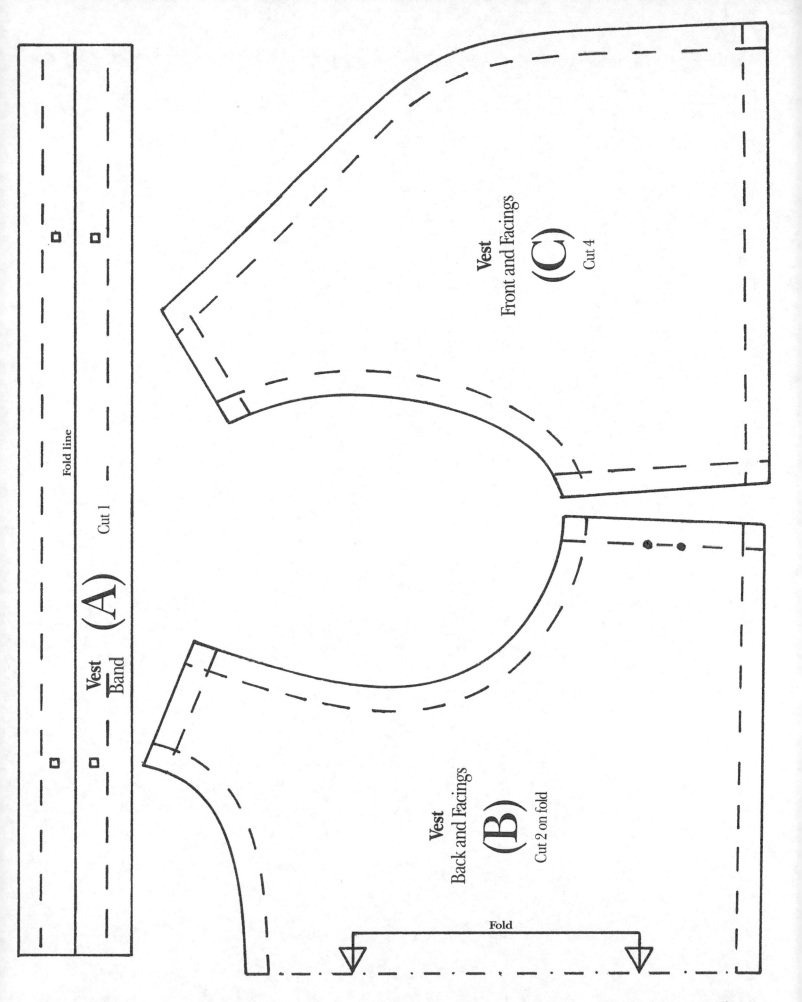

Fold line

Vest
Band **(A)**

Cut 1

Vest
Front and Facings
(C)
Cut 4

Vest
Back and Facings
(B)
Cut 2 on fold

Fold

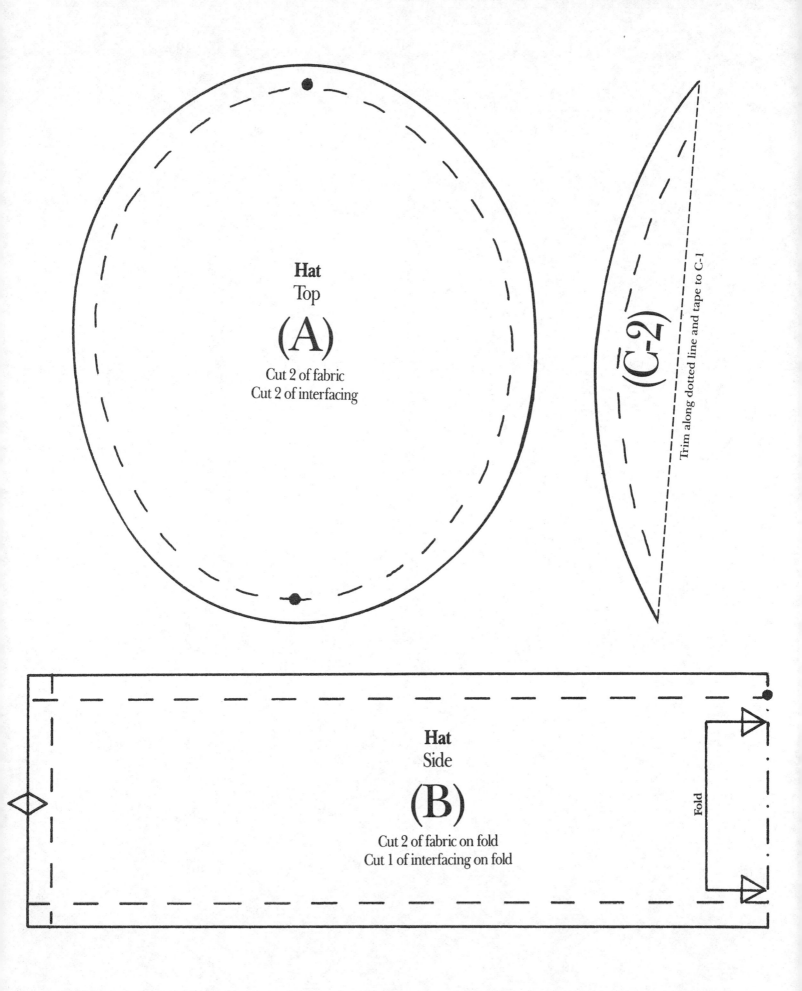

Hat
Top

(A)

Cut 2 of fabric
Cut 2 of interfacing

(C-2)

Trim along dotted line and tape to C-1

Hat
Side

(B)

Cut 2 of fabric on fold
Cut 1 of interfacing on fold

Fold

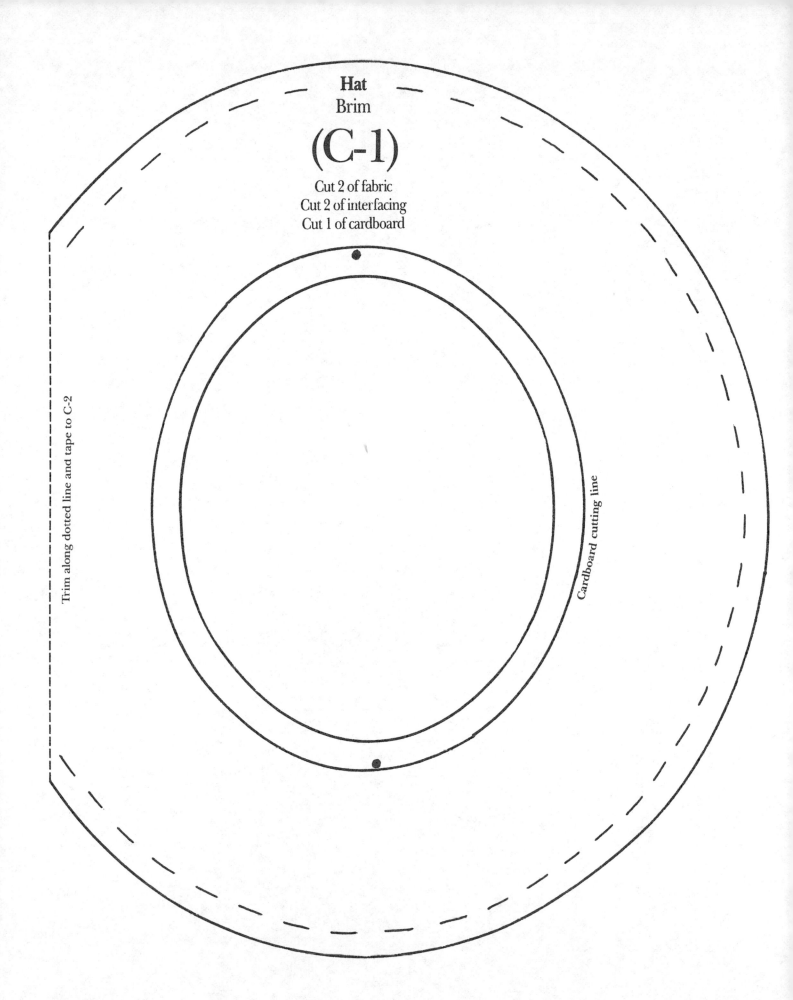

Hat
Brim

(C-1)

Cut 2 of fabric
Cut 2 of interfacing
Cut 1 of cardboard

Trim along dotted line and tape to C-2

Cardboard cutting line

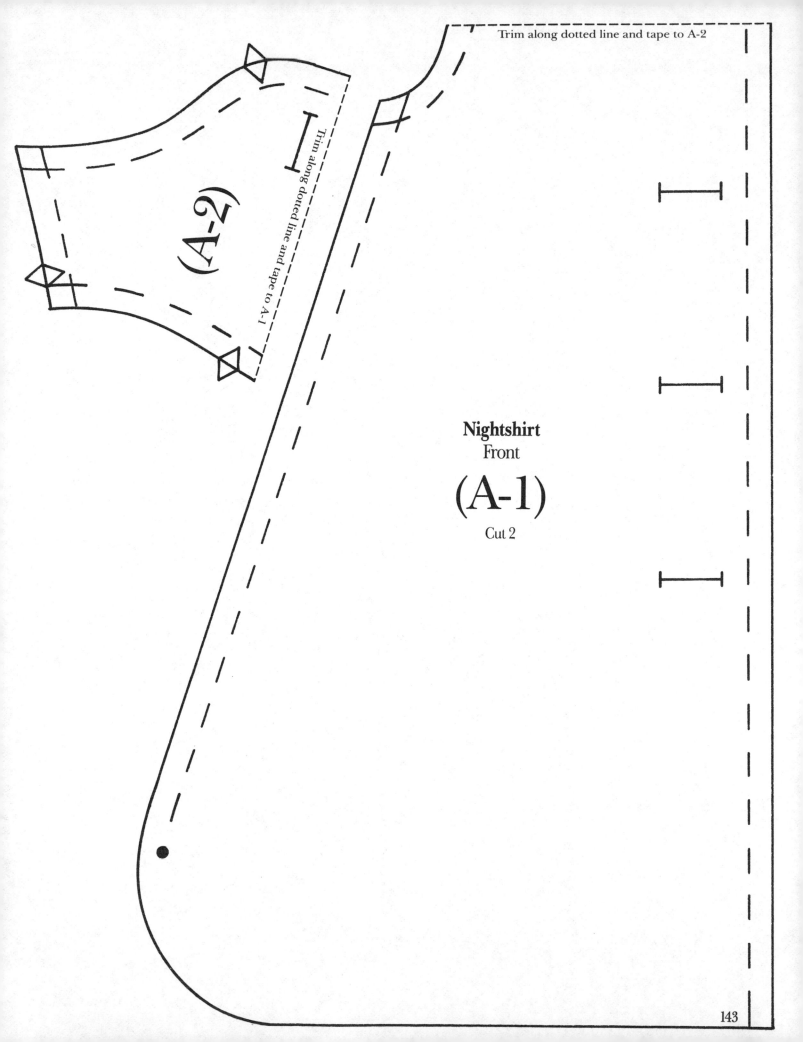

Trim along dotted line and tape to A-2

(A-2)

Trim along dotted line and tape to A-1

Nightshirt
Front

(A-1)

Cut 2

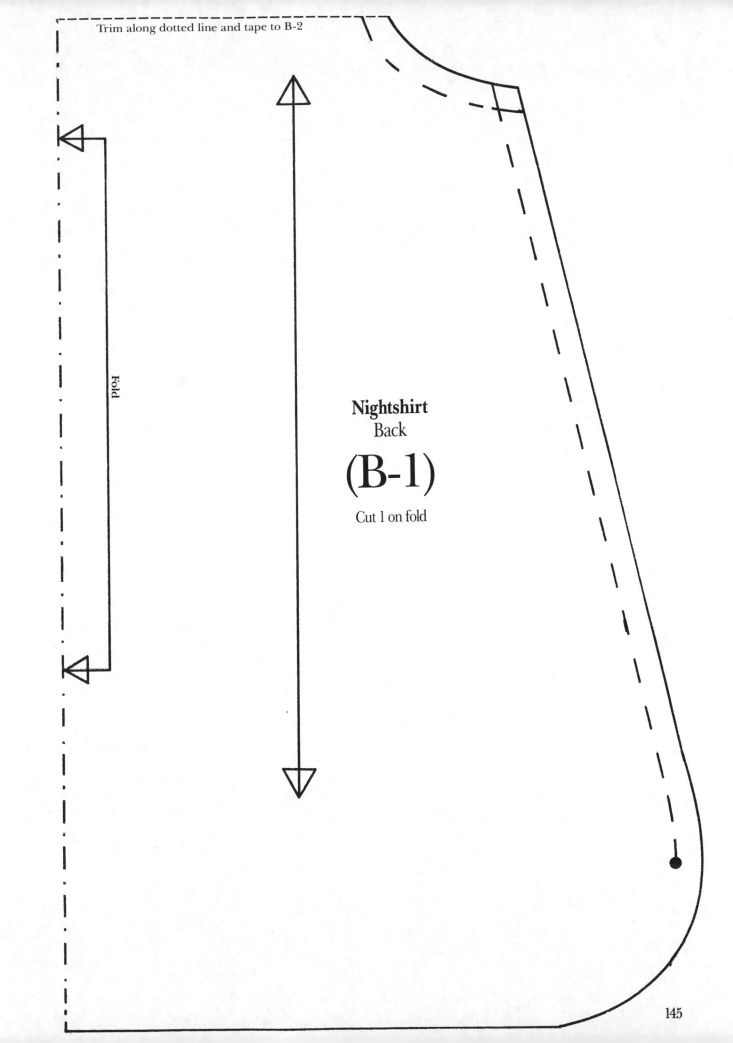

Trim along dotted line and tape to B-2

Fold

Nightshirt
Back

(B-1)

Cut 1 on fold

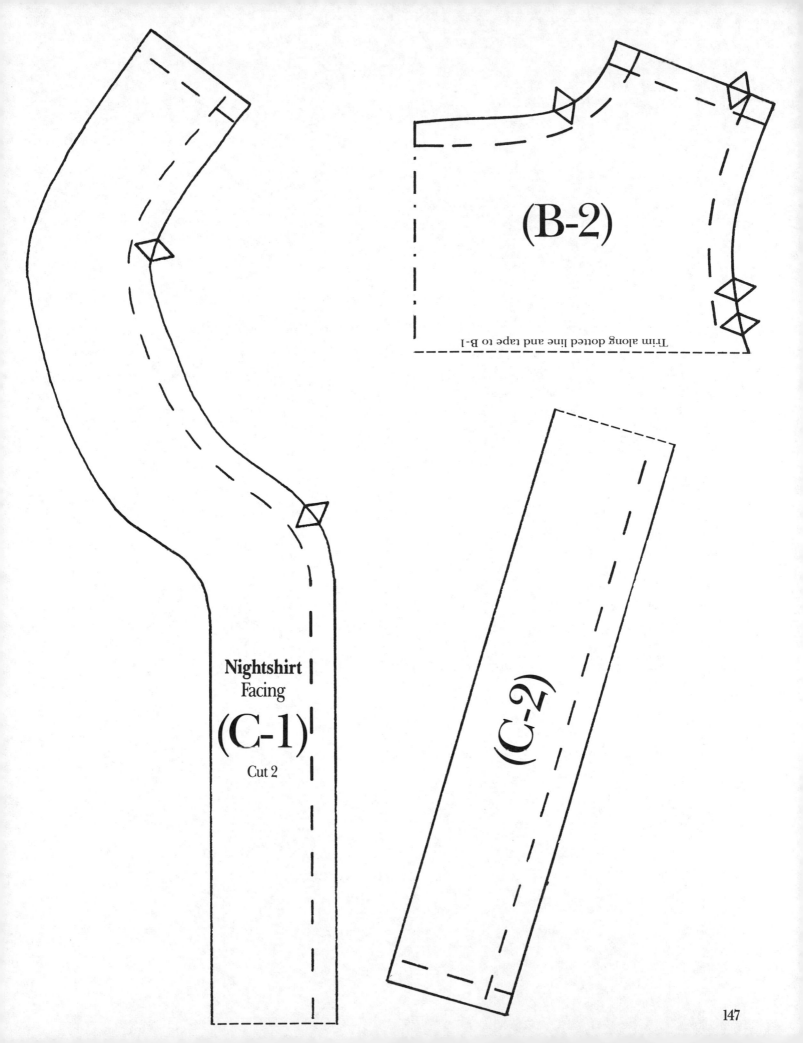

(B-2)

Trim along dotted line and tape to B-1

Nightshirt
Facing
(C-1)
Cut 2

(C-2)

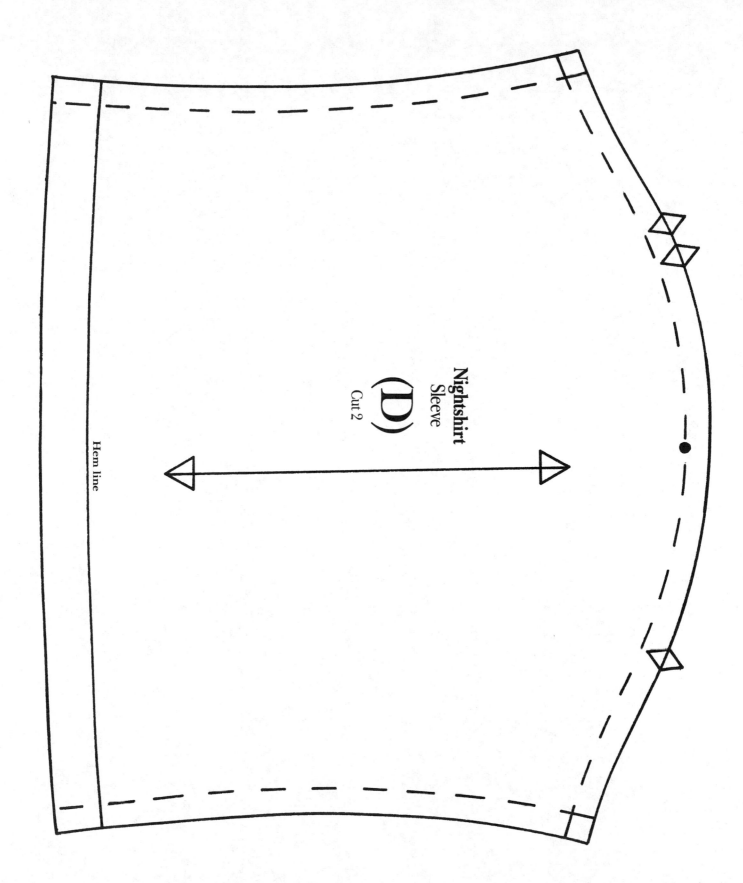

Nightshirt
Sleeve

(**D**)
Cut 2

Hem line

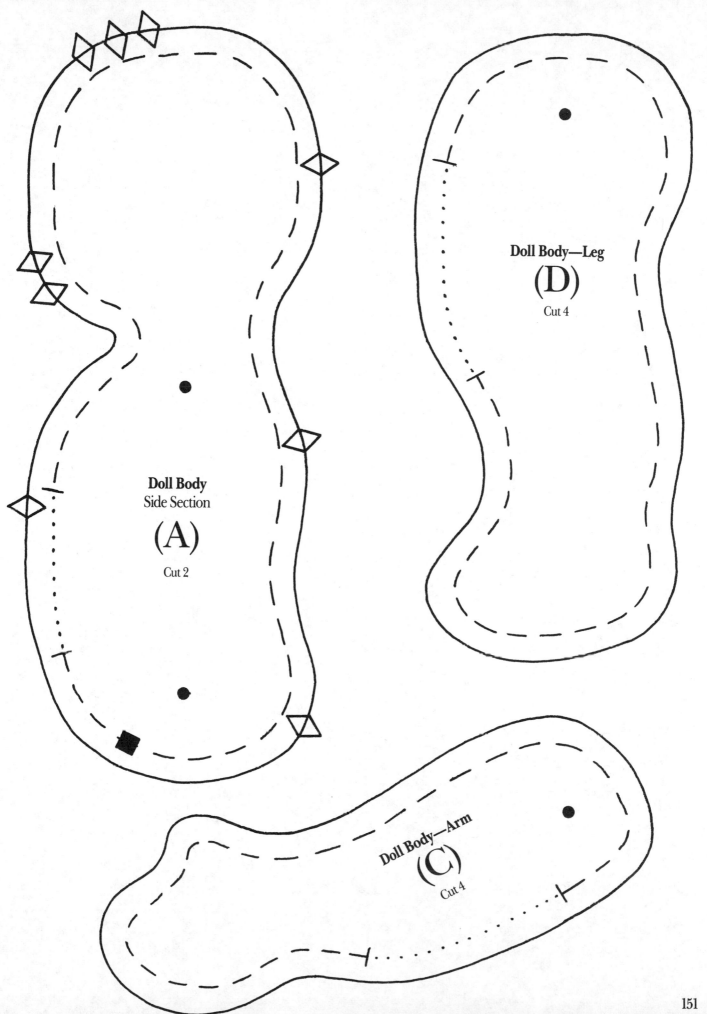

Doll Body
Side Section

(A)

Cut 2

Doll Body—Leg

(D)

Cut 4

Doll Body—Arm

(C)

Cut 4

151

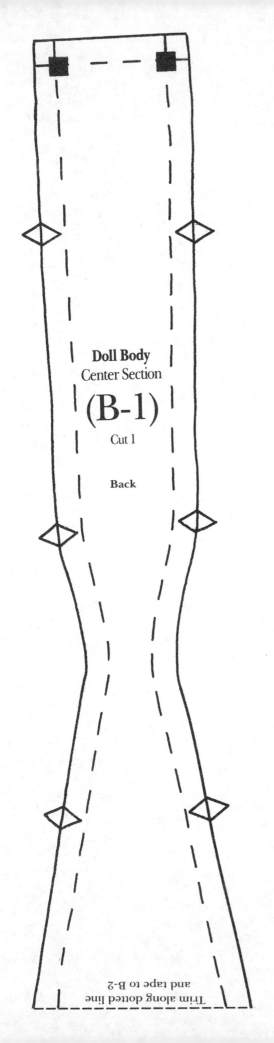

Doll Body
Center Section

(B-1)

Cut 1

Back

Trim along dotted line
and tape to B-2

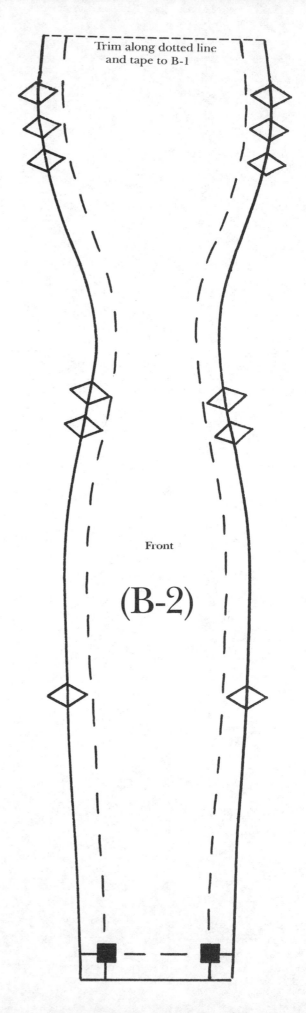

Trim along dotted line
and tape to B-1

Front

(B-2)

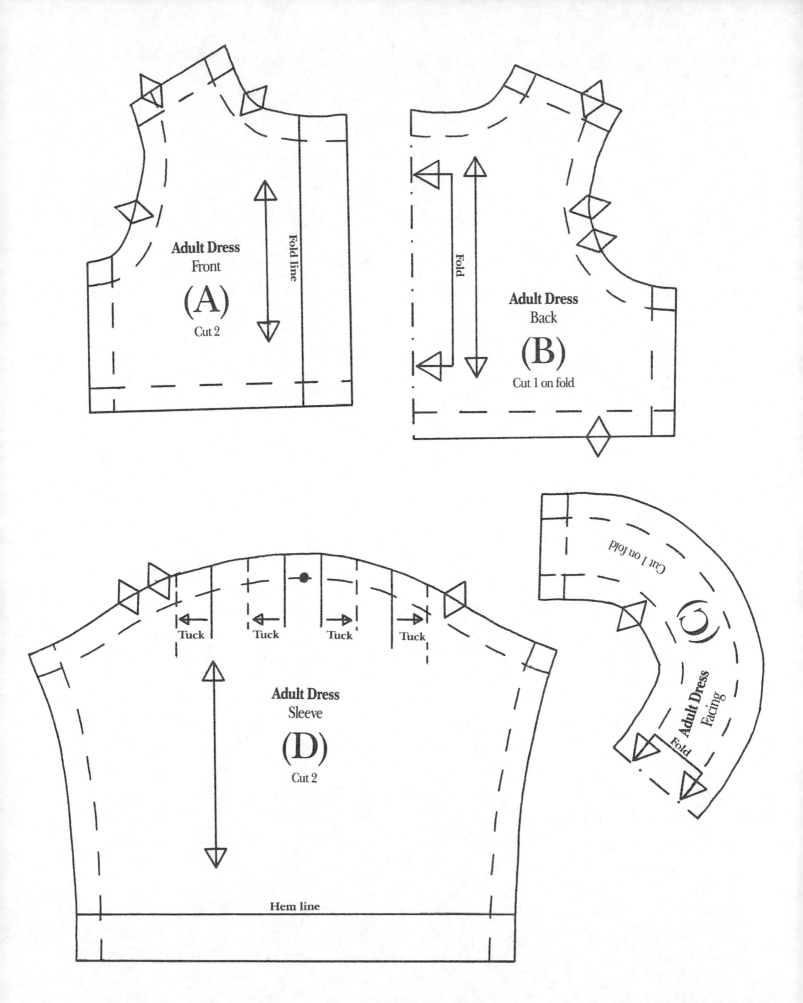

Adult Dress
Front

(A)

Cut 2

Fold line

Adult Dress
Back

(B)

Cut 1 on fold

Fold

Adult Dress
Sleeve

(D)

Cut 2

Tuck Tuck Tuck Tuck

Hem line

Cut 1 on fold

Adult Dress
Facing

(C)

Fold

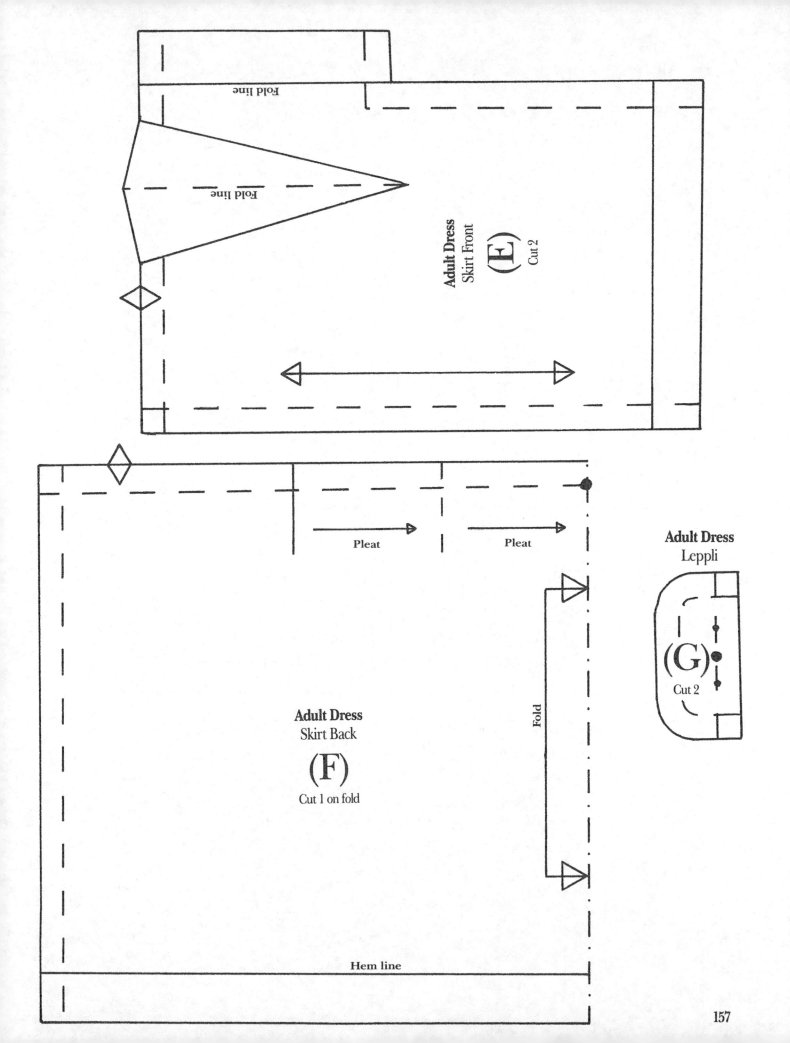

Fold line

Fold line

Adult Dress
Skirt Front

(E)

Cut 2

Adult Dress
Leppli

Pleat

Pleat

Adult Dress
Leppli

(G)

Cut 2

Adult Dress
Skirt Back

(F)

Cut 1 on fold

Fold

Hem line

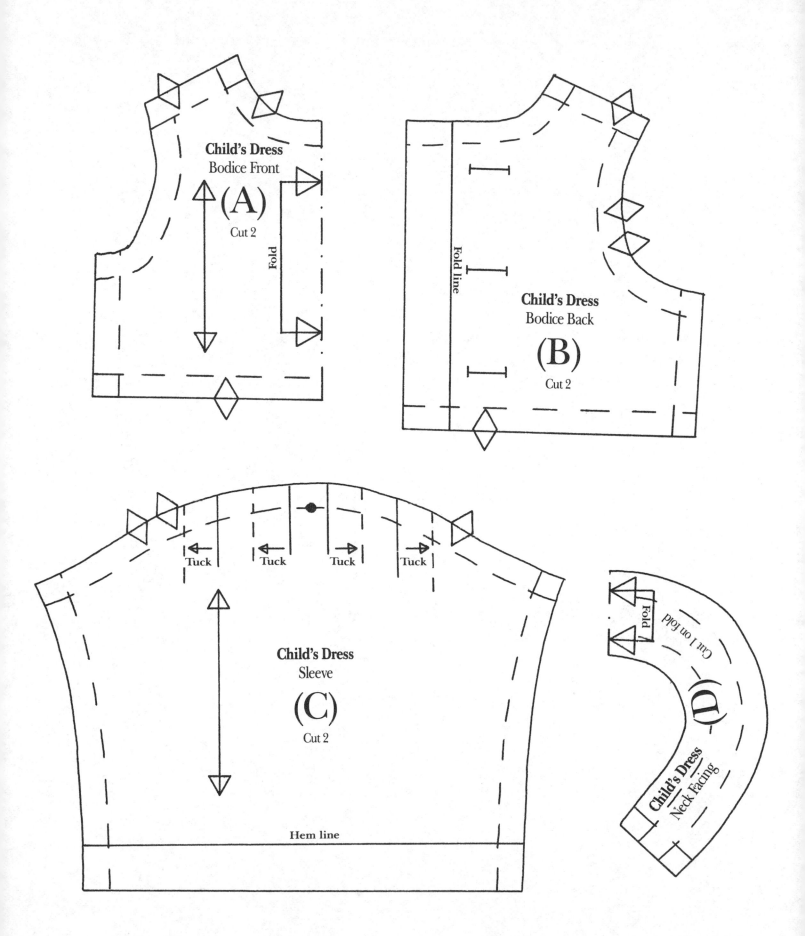

Child's Dress
Bodice Front

(A)

Cut 2

Fold

Child's Dress
Bodice Back

Fold line

(B)

Cut 2

Child's Dress
Sleeve

(C)

Cut 2

Tuck　Tuck　Tuck　Tuck

Hem line

Child's Dress
Neck Facing

(D)

Fold

Cut 1 on fold

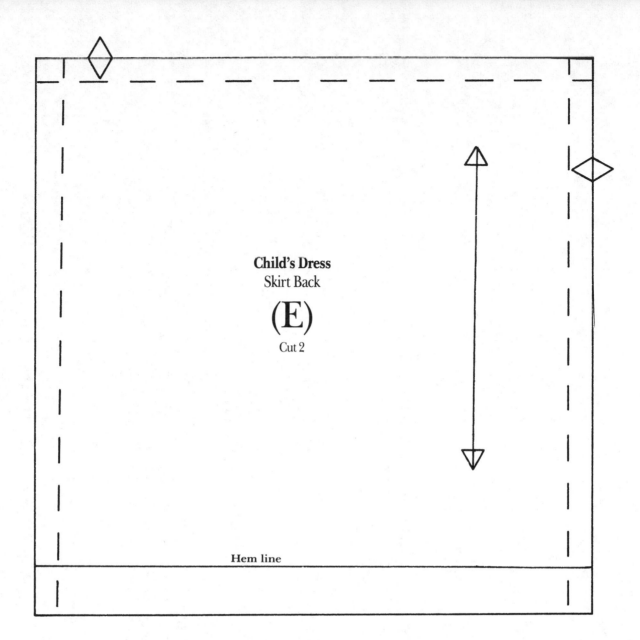

Child's Dress
Skirt Back

(E)

Cut 2

Hem line

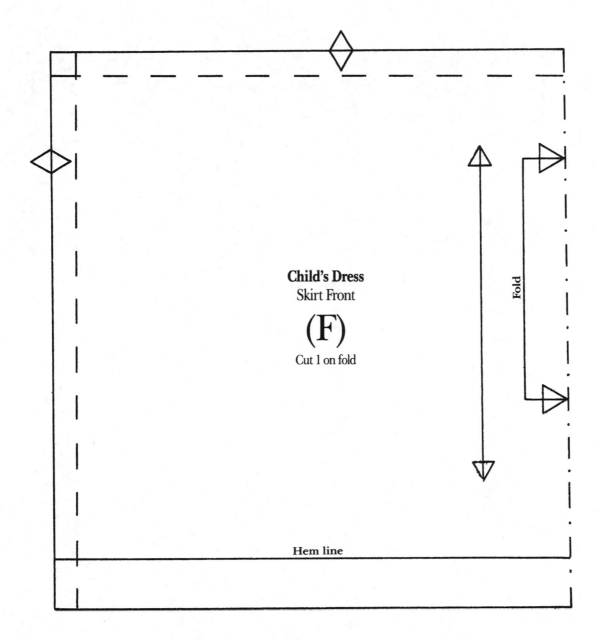

Child's Dress
Skirt Front

(F)

Cut 1 on fold

Fold

Hem line

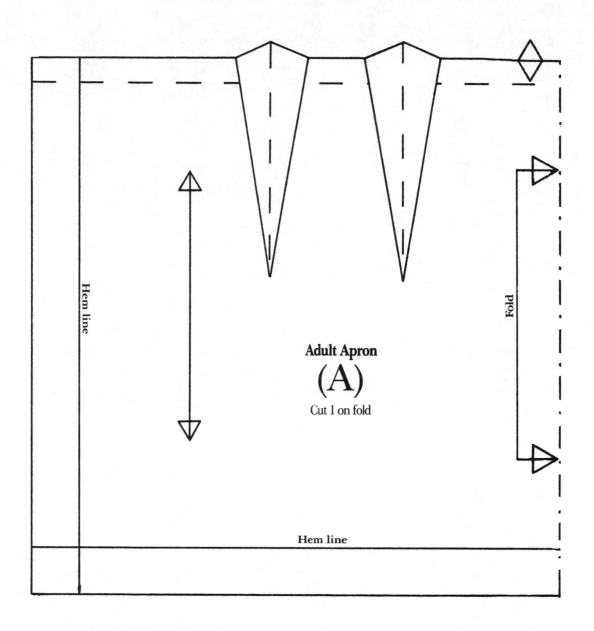

Adult Apron

(A)

Cut 1 on fold

Hem line

Hem line

Fold

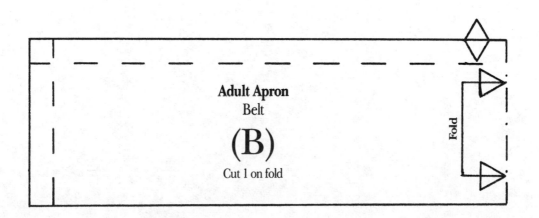

Adult Apron
Belt

(B)

Cut 1 on fold

Fold

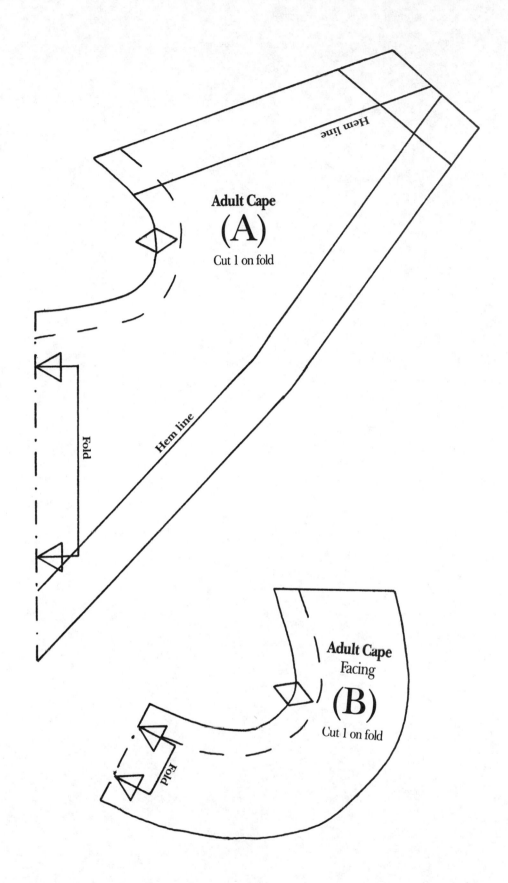

Adult Cape
(A)
Cut 1 on fold

Hem line

Hem line

Fold

Fold

Adult Cape
Facing
(B)
Cut 1 on fold

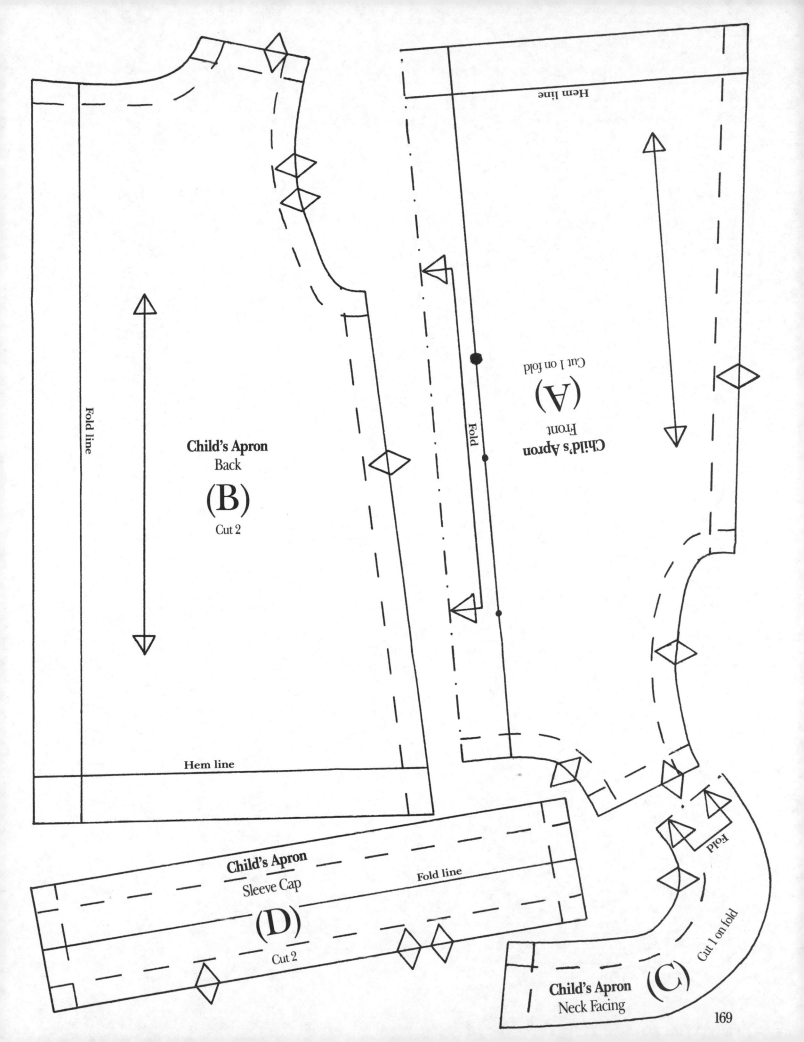

Child's Apron
Back

(B)

Cut 2

Fold line

Hem line

Child's Apron
Front

(A)

Cut 1 on fold

Fold

Hem line

Child's Apron
Sleeve Cap

(D)

Fold line

Cut 2

Child's Apron
Neck Facing

(C)

Cut 1 on fold

Fold

169

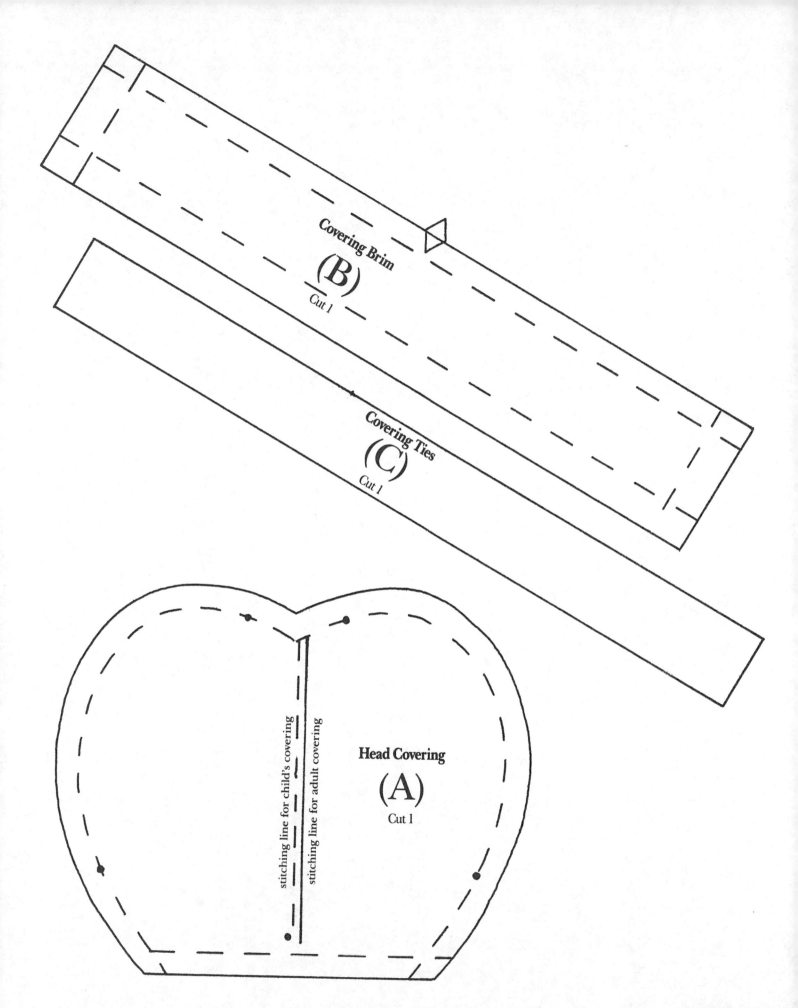

Covering Brim

(B)

Cut 1

Covering Ties

(C)

Cut 1

stitching line for child's covering

stitching line for adult covering

Head Covering

(A)

Cut 1

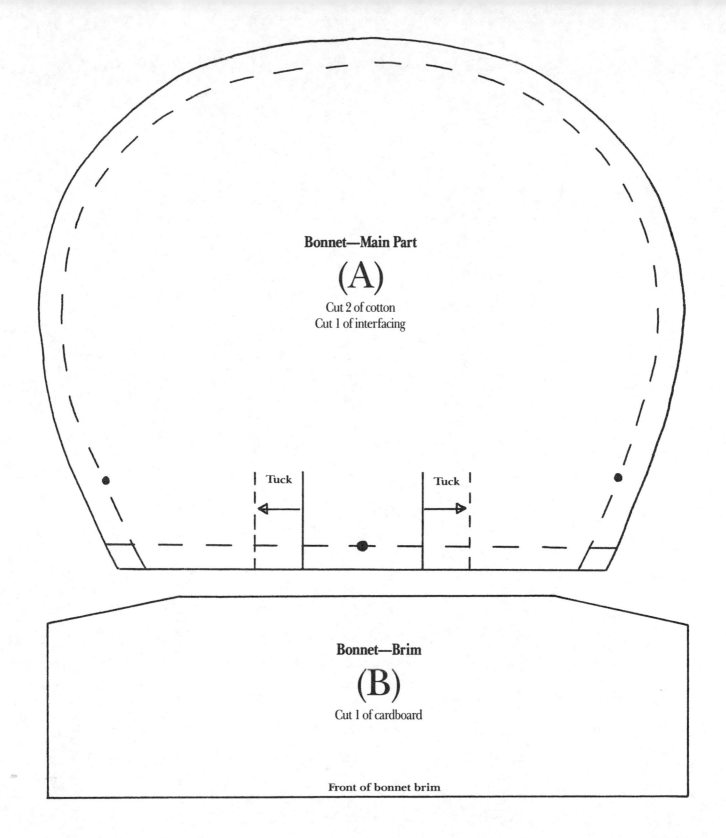

Bonnet—Main Part

(A)

Cut 2 of cotton
Cut 1 of interfacing

Tuck

Tuck

Bonnet—Brim

(B)

Cut 1 of cardboard

Front of bonnet brim

Bonnet—Binding Strip

(C)

Cut 1

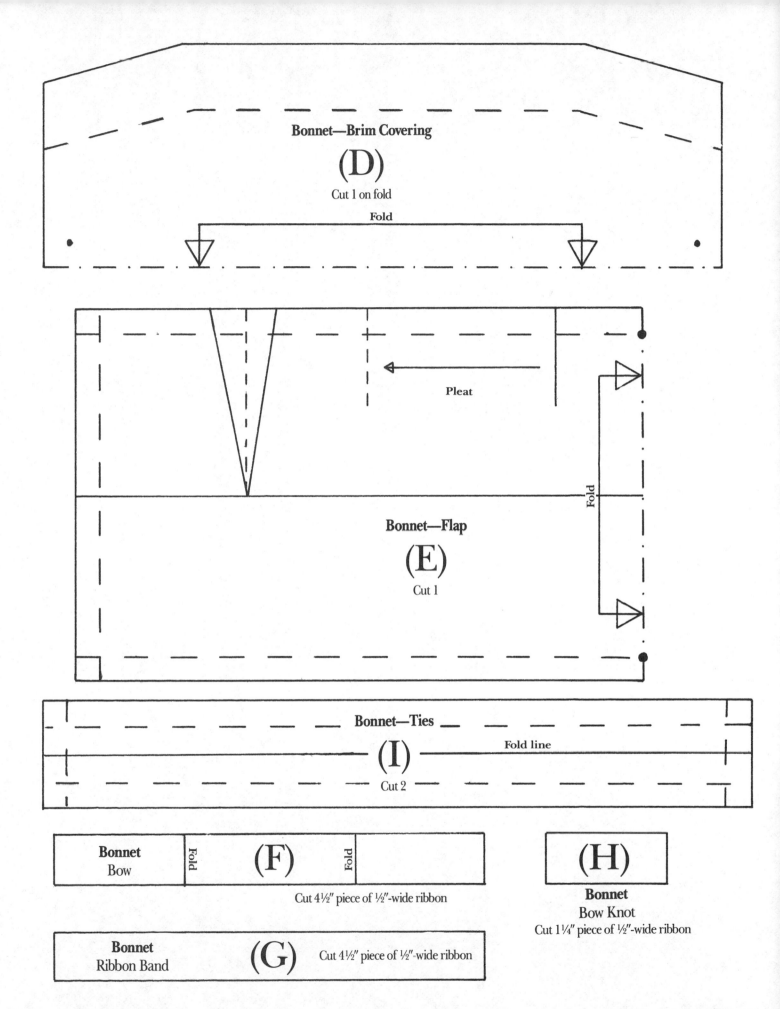

Bonnet—Brim Covering

(D)

Cut 1 on fold

Fold

Bonnet—Flap

(E)

Cut 1

Pleat

Fold

Bonnet—Ties

(I)

Fold line

Cut 2

Bonnet
Bow

Fold

(F)

Fold

Cut 4½″ piece of ½″-wide ribbon

(H)

Bonnet
Bow Knot
Cut 1¼″ piece of ½″-wide ribbon

Bonnet
Ribbon Band

(G)

Cut 4½″ piece of ½″-wide ribbon

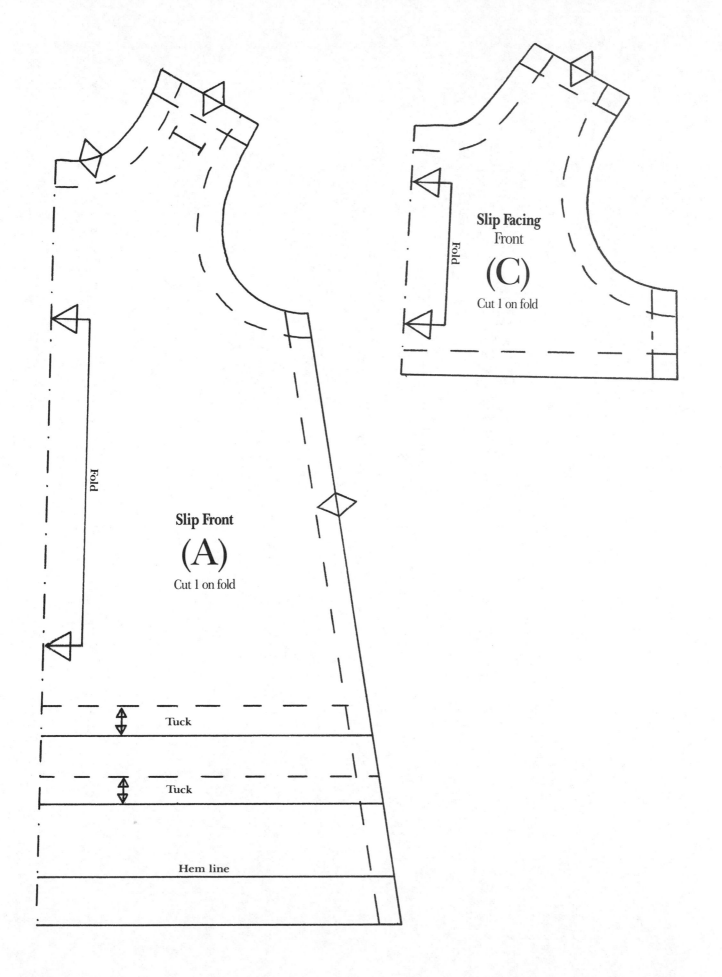

Slip Front

(A)

Cut 1 on fold

Fold

Tuck

Tuck

Hem line

Slip Facing
Front

(C)

Cut 1 on fold

Fold

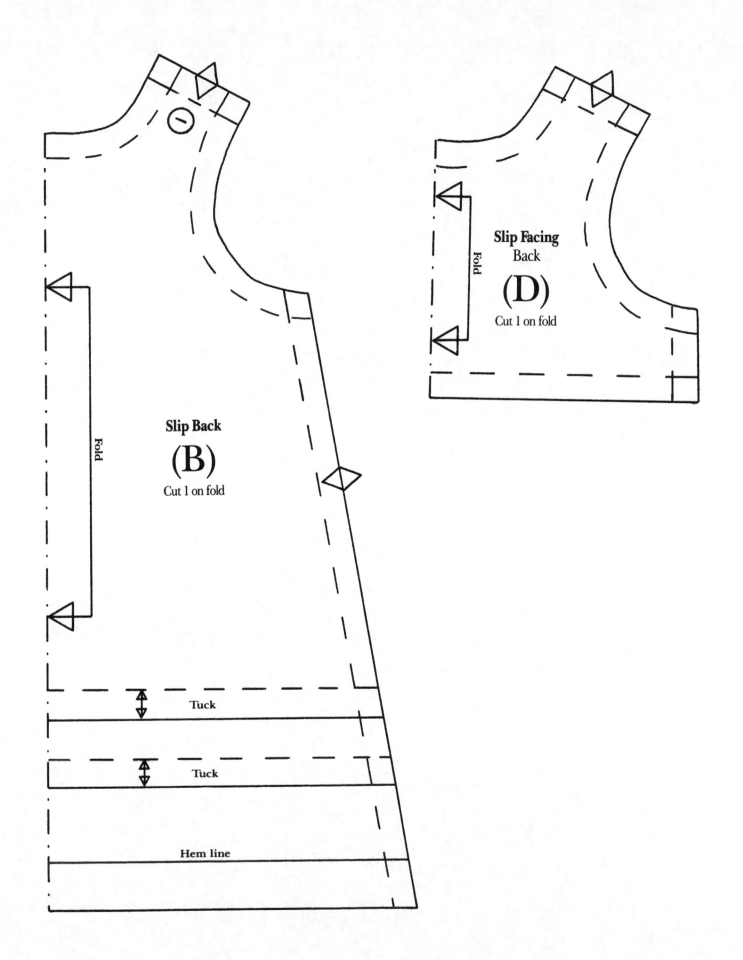

Slip Back

(B)

Cut 1 on fold

Fold

Tuck

Tuck

Hem line

Slip Facing
Back

(D)

Cut 1 on fold

Fold

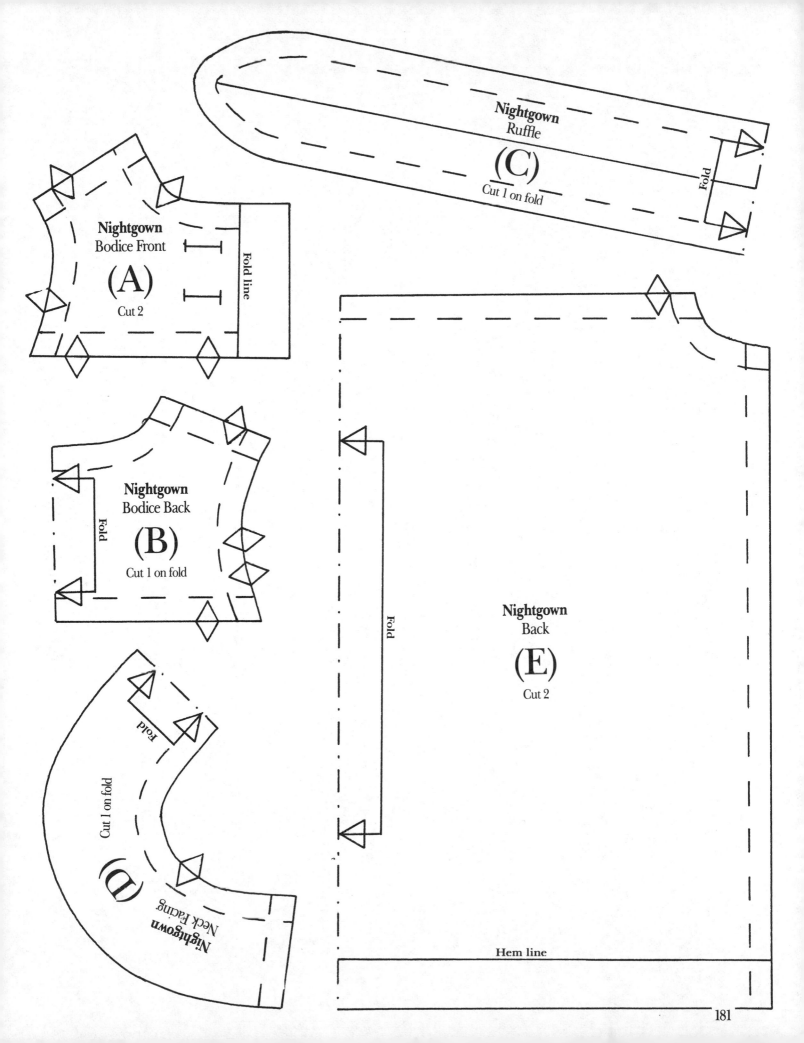

Nightgown
Ruffle

(C)
Cut 1 on fold

Fold

Nightgown
Bodice Front

(A)
Cut 2

Fold line

Nightgown
Bodice Back

(B)
Cut 1 on fold

Fold

Nightgown
Back

(E)
Cut 2

Fold

Cut 1 on fold

(D)
Fold

Nightgown
Neck Facing

Hem line

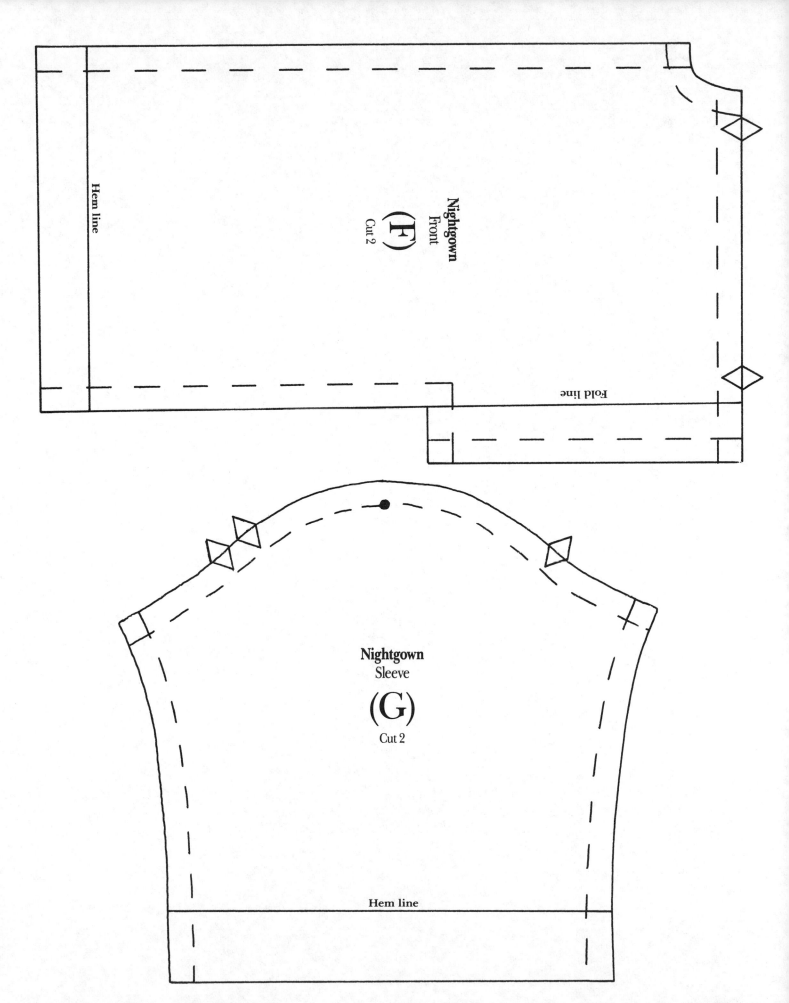

Nightgown
Front

(F)
Cut 2

Hem line

Fold line

Nightgown
Sleeve

(G)

Cut 2

Hem line

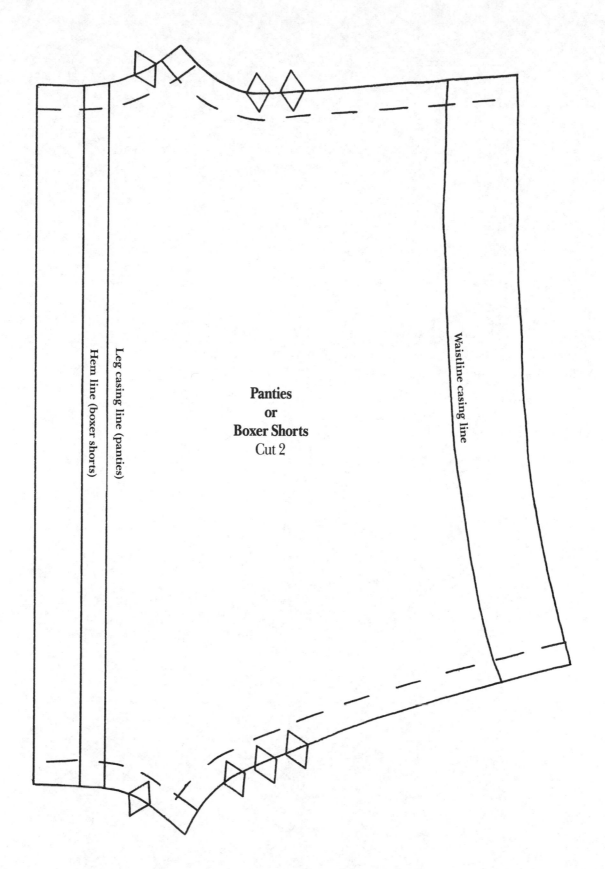

Hem line (boxer shorts)

Leg casing line (panties)

Waistline casing line

Panties
or
Boxer Shorts
Cut 2

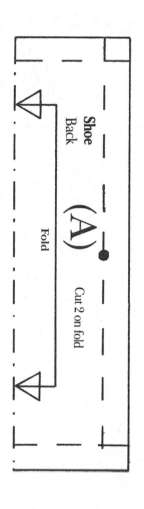

Shoe
Back

(A)

Fold

Cut 2 on fold

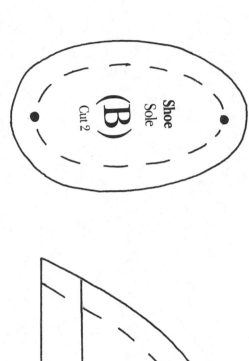

Shoe
Sole

(B)

Cut 2

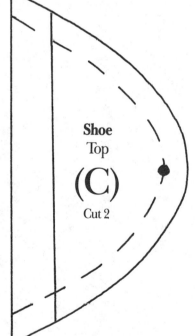

Shoe
Top

(C)

Cut 2

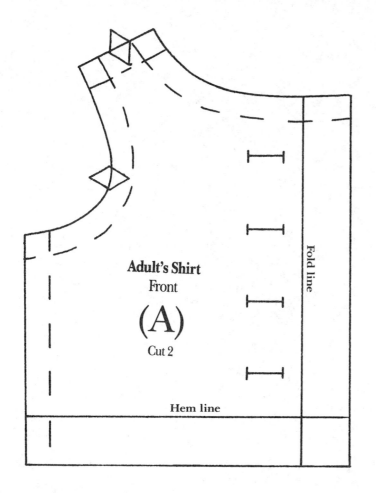

Adult's Shirt
Front

(A)

Cut 2

Fold line

Hem line

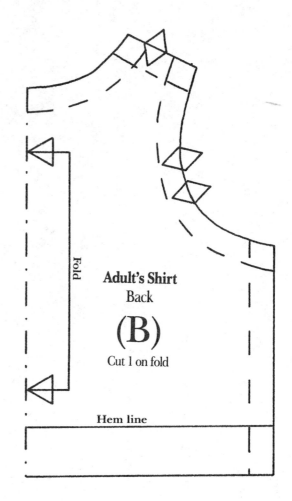

Adult's Shirt
Back

(B)

Cut 1 on fold

Fold

Hem line

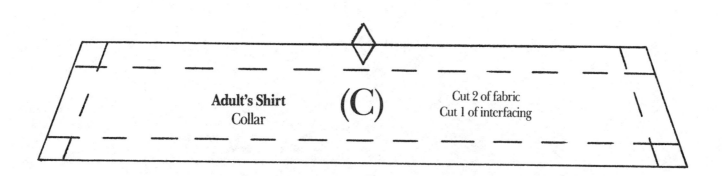

Adult's Shirt
Collar

(C)

Cut 2 of fabric
Cut 1 of interfacing

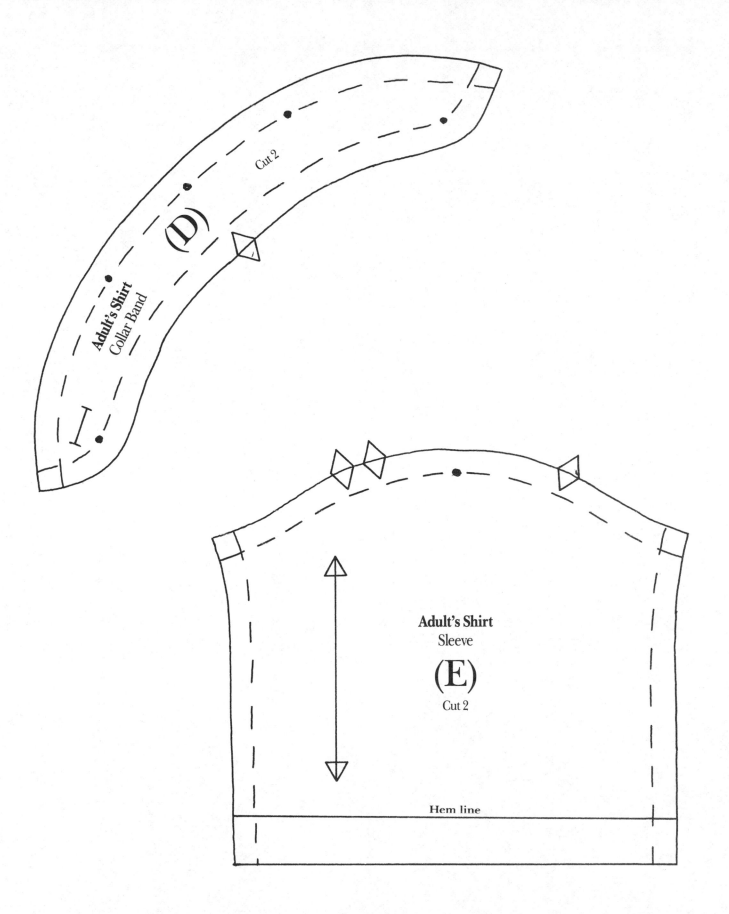

Adult's Shirt
Collar Band

Cut 2

(D)

Adult's Shirt
Sleeve

(E)

Cut 2

Hem line

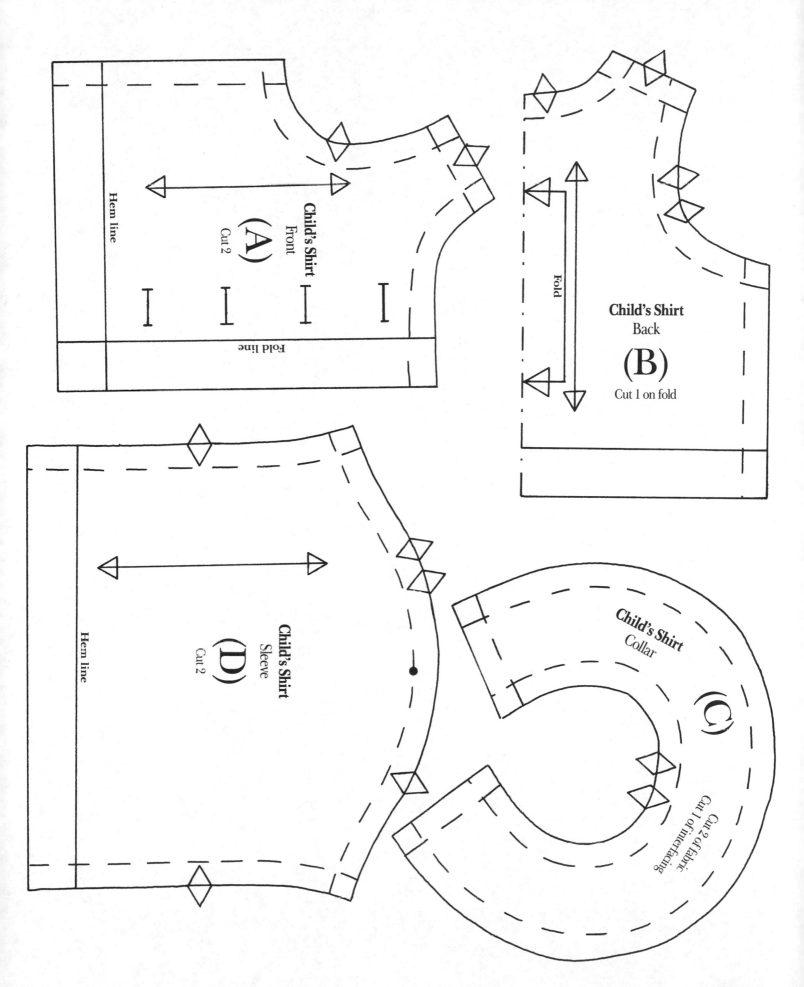

Child's Shirt
Front

(A)
Cut 2

Hem line

Fold line

Child's Shirt
Back

(B)
Cut 1 on fold

Fold

Child's Shirt
Sleeve

(D)
Cut 2

Hem line

Child's Shirt
Collar

(C)

Cut 1 of fabric
Cut 2 of fabric
Cut 1 of interfacing

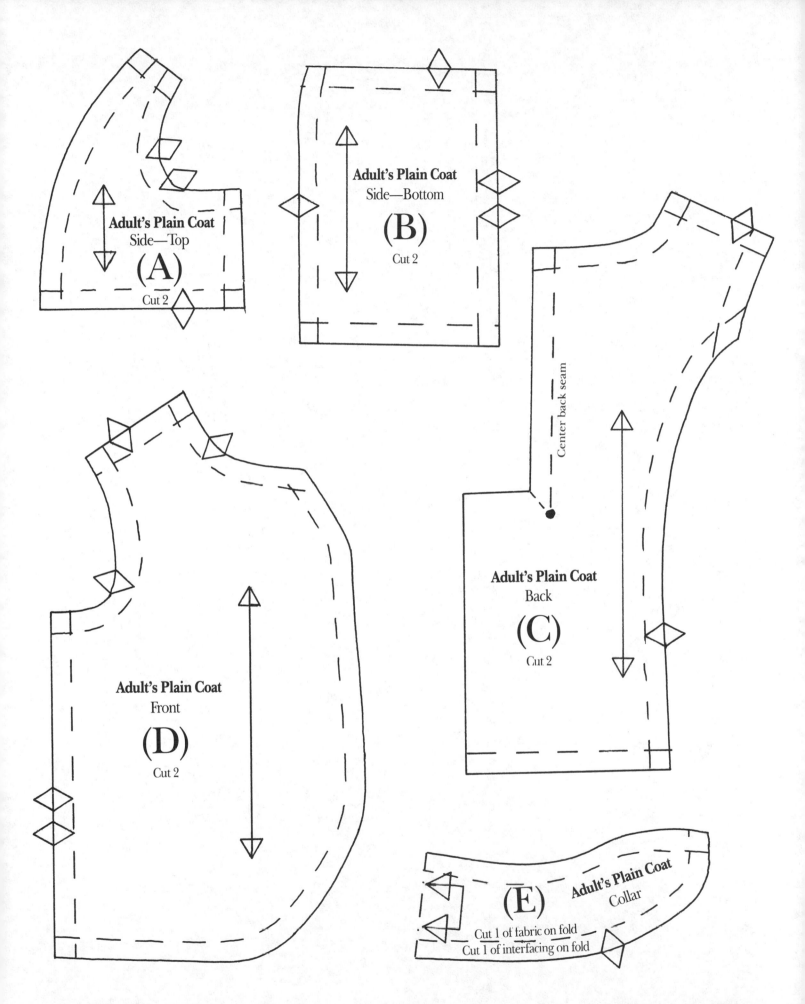

Adult's Plain Coat
Side—Top

(A)

Cut 2

Adult's Plain Coat
Side—Bottom

(B)

Cut 2

Center back seam

Adult's Plain Coat
Back

(C)

Cut 2

Adult's Plain Coat
Front

(D)

Cut 2

(E) **Adult's Plain Coat**
Collar

Cut 1 of fabric on fold
Cut 1 of interfacing on fold

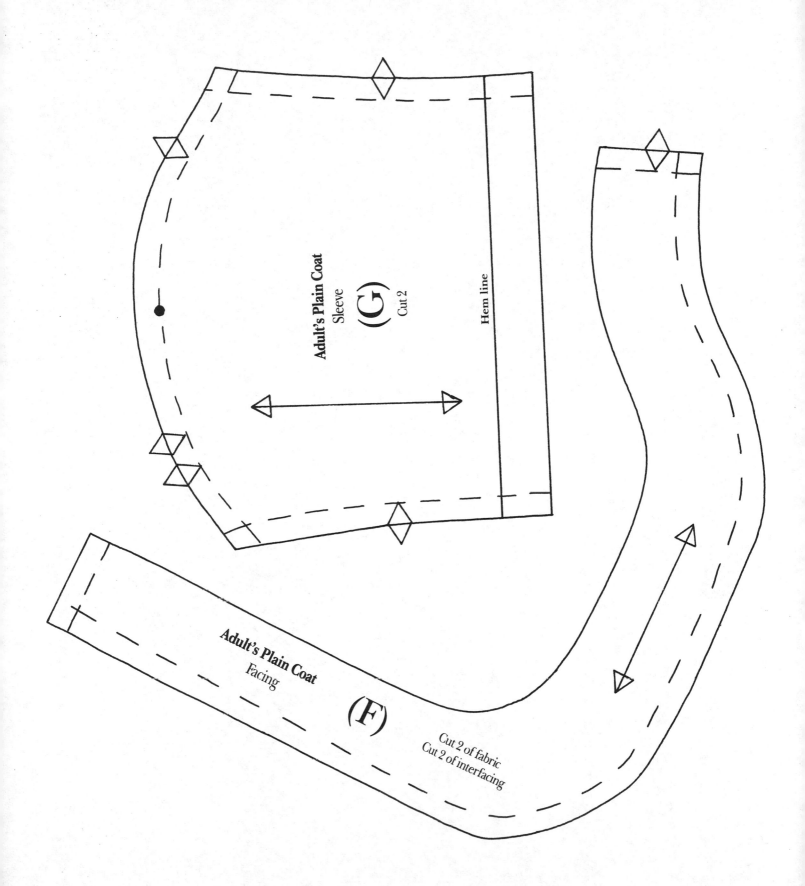

Adult's Plain Coat
Sleeve
(G)
Cut 2

Hem line

Adult's Plain Coat
Facing

(F)

Cut 2 of fabric
Cut 2 of interfacing

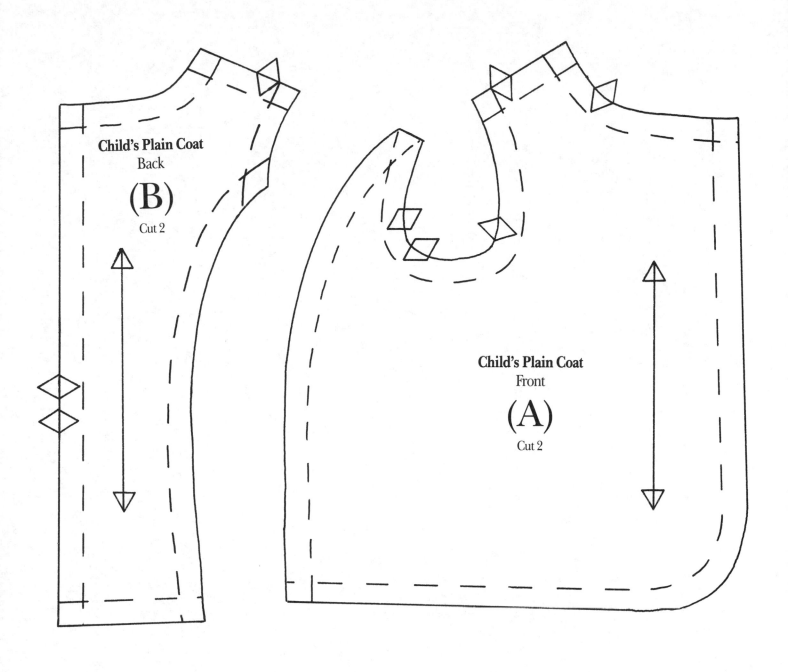

Child's Plain Coat
Back

(B)

Cut 2

Child's Plain Coat
Front

(A)

Cut 2

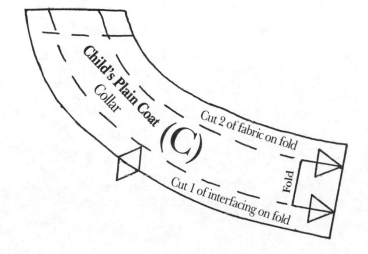

Child's Plain Coat
Collar
(C)
Cut 2 of fabric on fold
Cut 1 of interfacing on fold
Fold

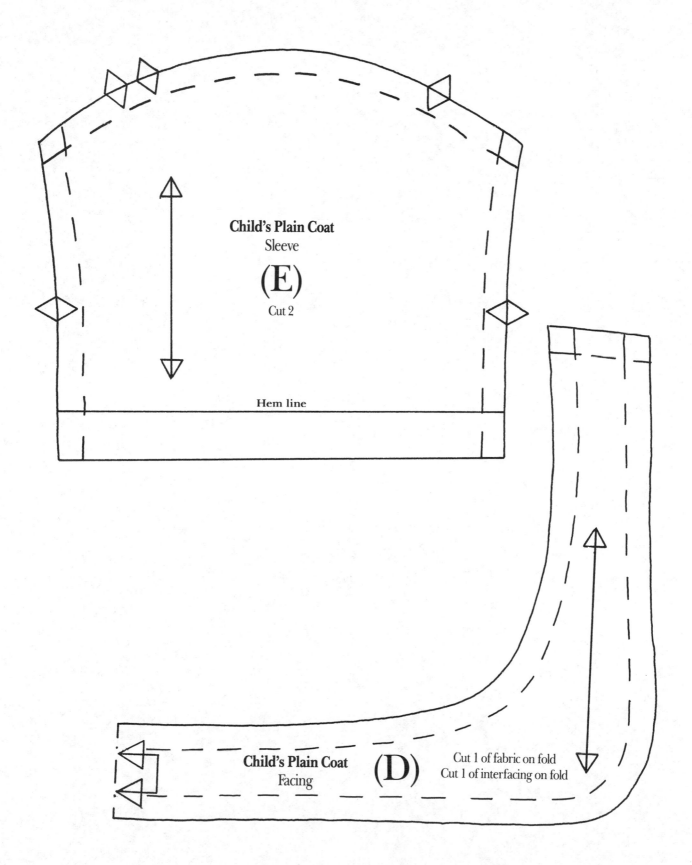

Child's Plain Coat
Sleeve

(E)

Cut 2

Hem line

Child's Plain Coat
Facing

(D)

Cut 1 of fabric on fold
Cut 1 of interfacing on fold

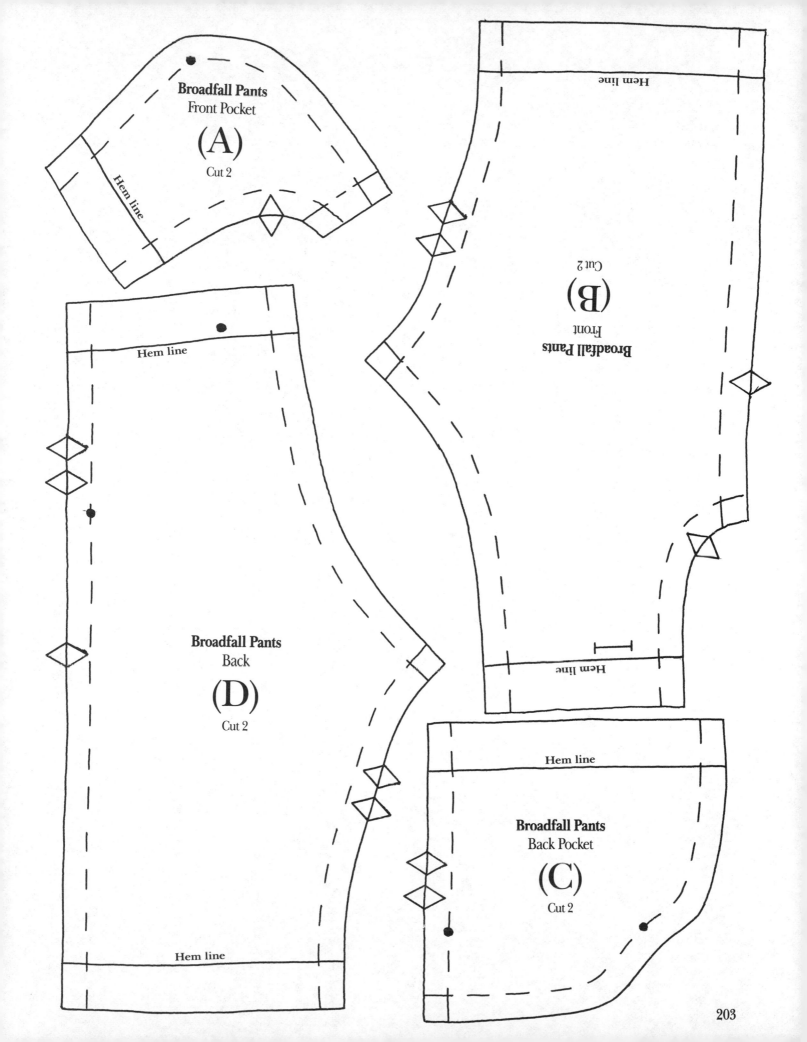

Broadfall Pants
Front Pocket

(A)

Cut 2

Hem line

Hem line

Broadfall Pants

(B)

Front

Cut 2

Hem line

Hem line

Hem line

Broadfall Pants
Back

(D)

Cut 2

Hem line

Hem line

Broadfall Pants
Back Pocket

(C)

Cut 2

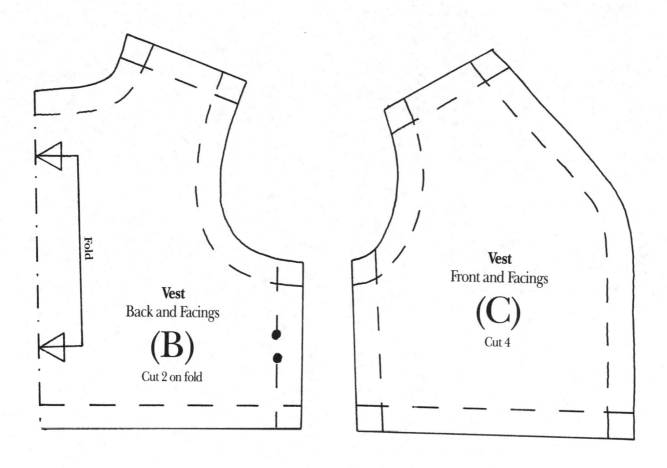

Vest
Back and Facings

(B)

Cut 2 on fold

Fold

Vest
Front and Facings

(C)

Cut 4

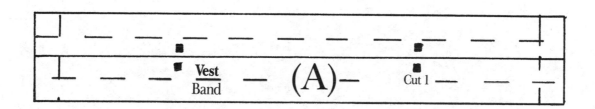

Vest
Band

(A)

Cut 1

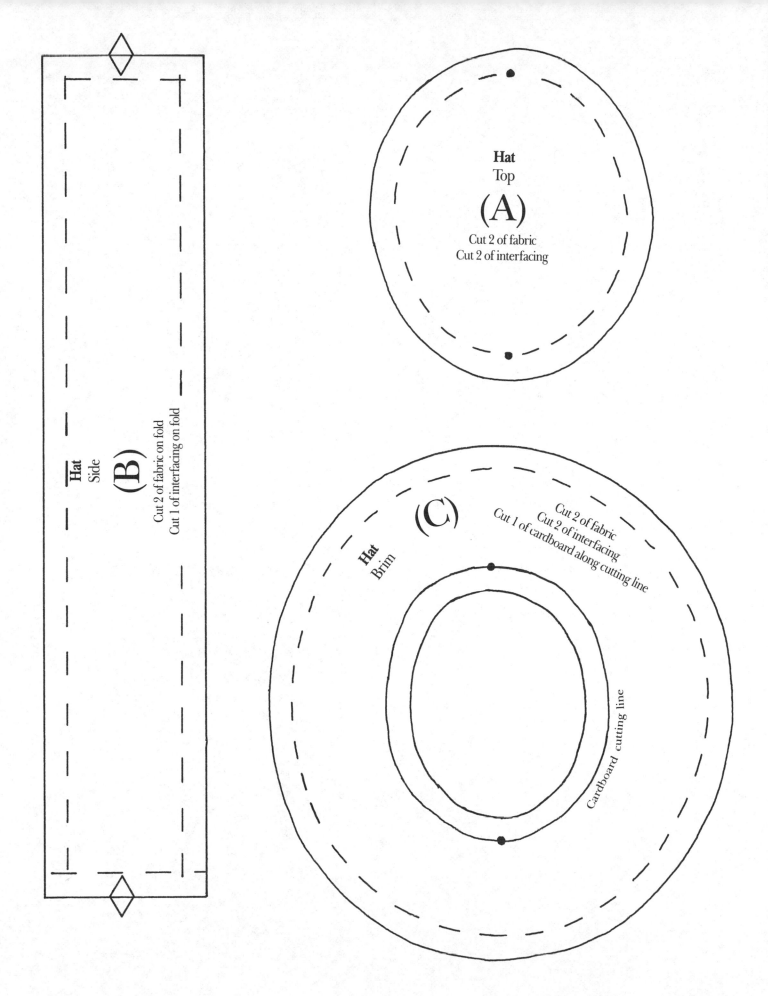

Hat
Top

(A)

Cut 2 of fabric
Cut 2 of interfacing

Hat
Side

(B)

Cut 2 of fabric on fold
Cut 1 of interfacing on fold

(C)

Cut 2 of fabric
Cut 2 of interfacing
Cut 1 of cardboard along cutting line

Hat
Brim

Cardboard cutting line

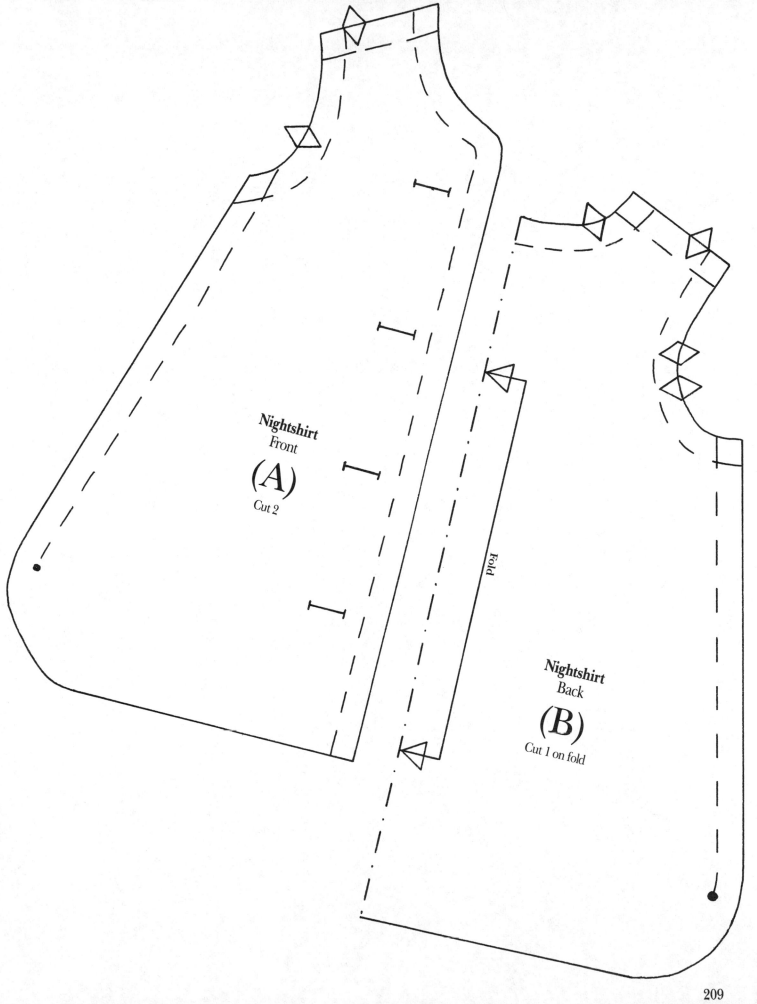

Nightshirt
Front

(A)

Cut 2

Fold

Nightshirt
Back

(B)

Cut 1 on fold

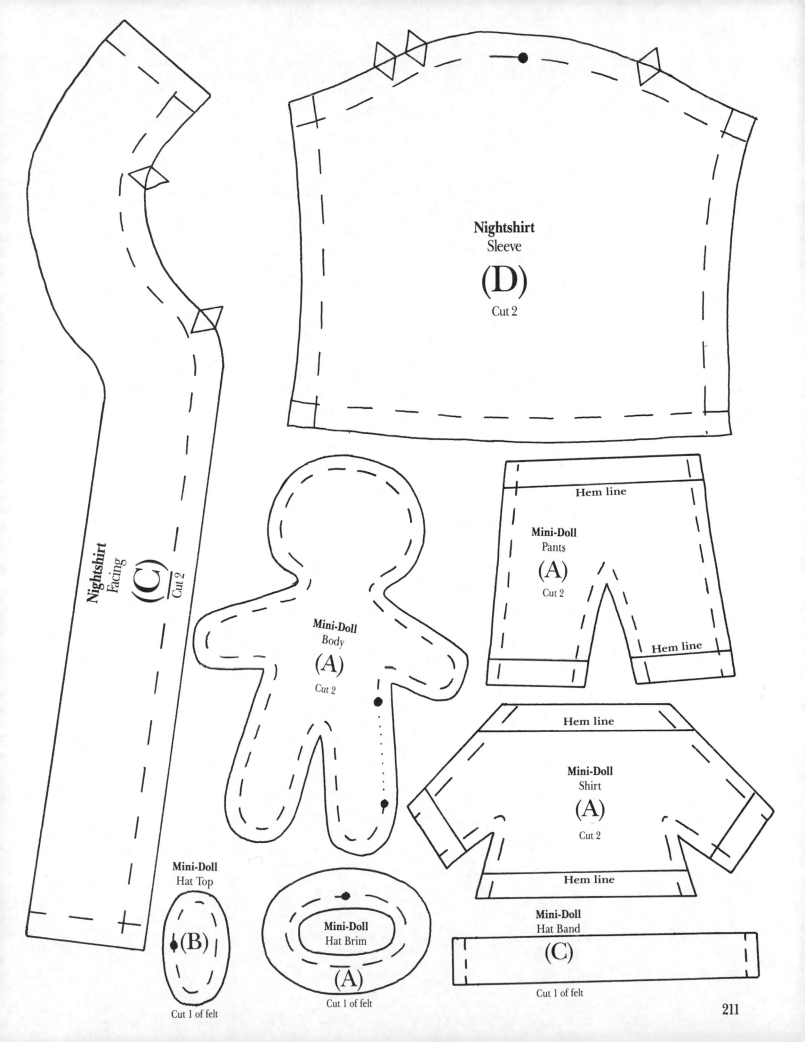

Nightshirt
Sleeve

(D)

Cut 2

Nightshirt Facing

(C)
Cut 2

Mini-Doll
Body

(A)

Cut 2

Mini-Doll
Pants

(A)

Cut 2

Hem line

Hem line

Hem line

Mini-Doll
Shirt

(A)

Cut 2

Hem line

Mini-Doll
Hat Top

(B)

Cut 1 of felt

Mini-Doll
Hat Brim

(A)

Cut 1 of felt

Mini-Doll
Hat Band

(C)

Cut 1 of felt

211

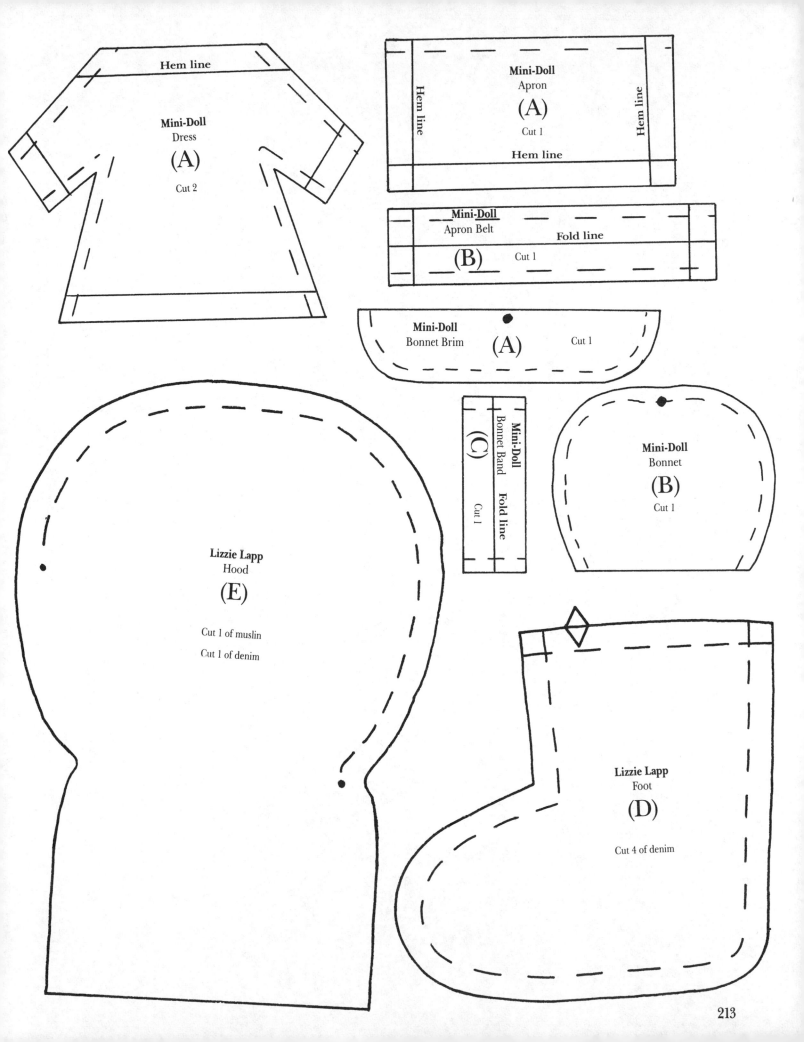

Hem line

Mini-Doll
Dress

(A)

Cut 2

Mini-Doll
Apron

(A)

Cut 1

Hem line

Hem line

Hem line

Mini-Doll
Apron Belt **Fold line**

(B) Cut 1

Mini-Doll
Bonnet Brim **(A)** Cut 1

Mini-Doll
Bonnet Band **Fold line**

(C) Cut 1

Mini-Doll
Bonnet

(B)

Cut 1

Lizzie Lapp
Hood

(E)

Cut 1 of muslin

Cut 1 of denim

Lizzie Lapp
Foot

(D)

Cut 4 of denim

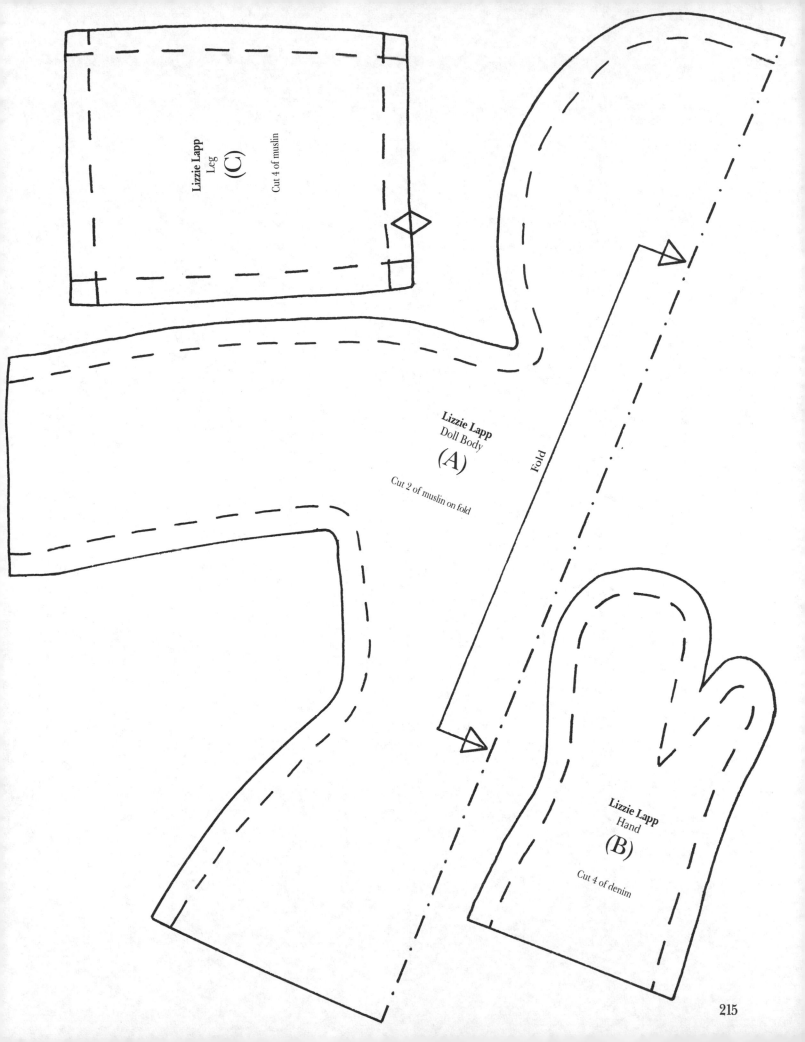

Lizzie Lapp
Leg
(C)

Cut 4 of muslin

Lizzie Lapp
Doll Body
(A)

Cut 2 of muslin on fold

Fold

Lizzie Lapp
Hand
(B)

Cut 4 of denim

215

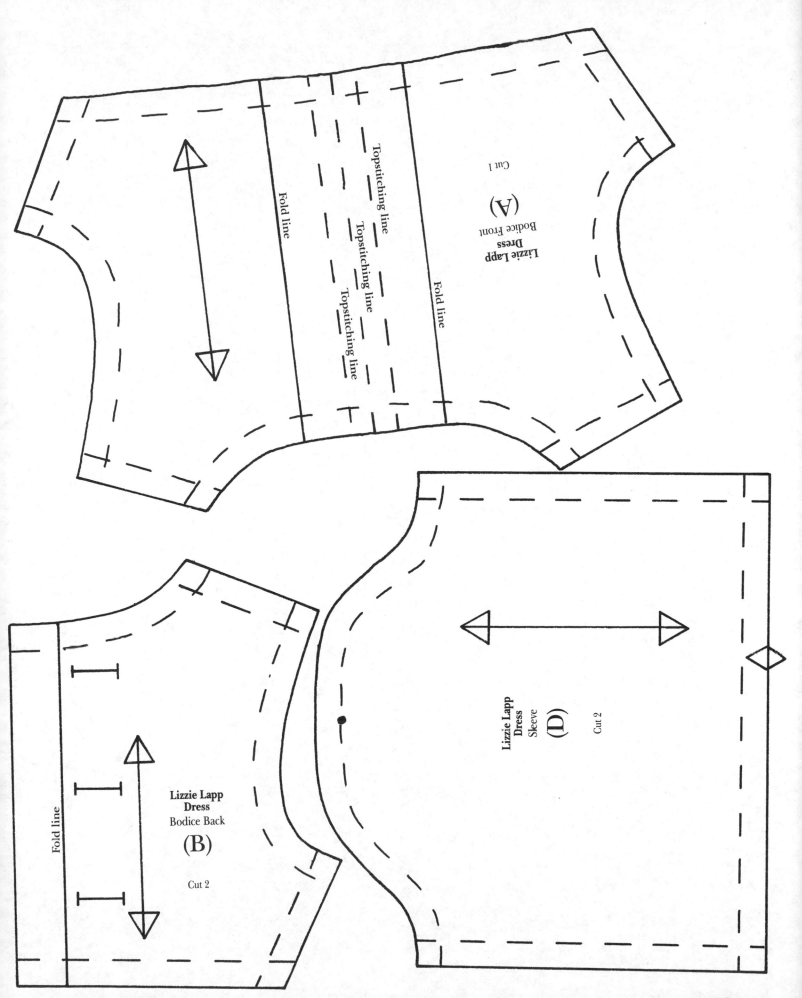

Topstitching line

Topstitching line

Topstitching line

Topstitching line

Fold line

Fold line

Cut 1

(A)

Lizzie Lapp
Dress
Bodice Front

Fold line

**Lizzie Lapp
Dress**
Bodice Back

(B)

Cut 2

**Lizzie Lapp
Dress**
Sleeve

(D)

Cut 2

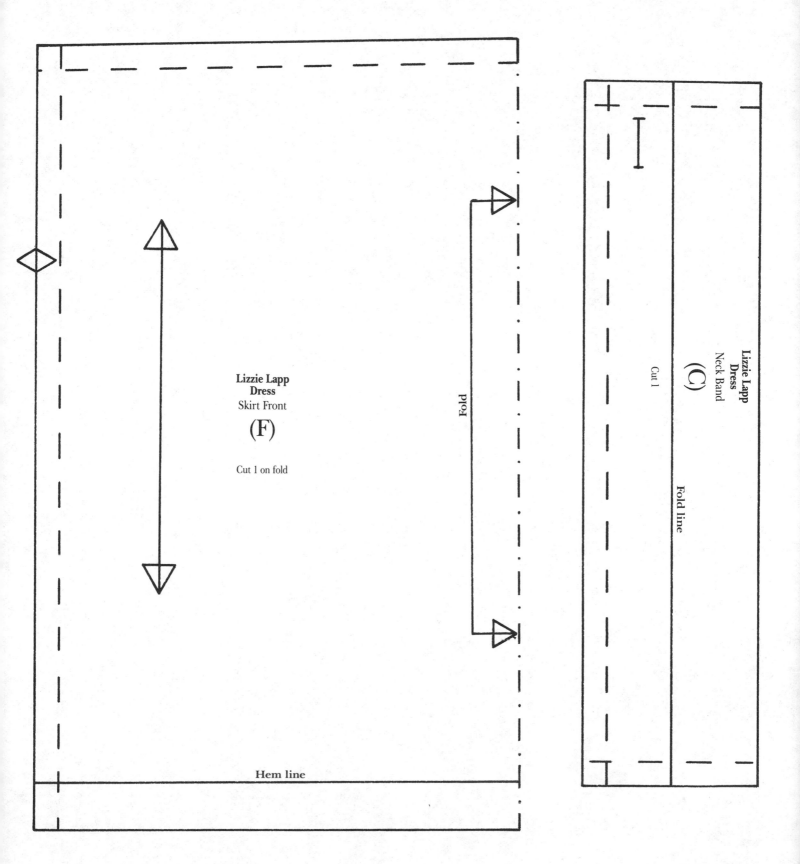

Lizzie Lapp
Dress
Skirt Front

(F)

Cut 1 on fold

Fold

Hem line

Lizzie Lapp
Dress
Neck Band

(C)

Cut 1

Fold line

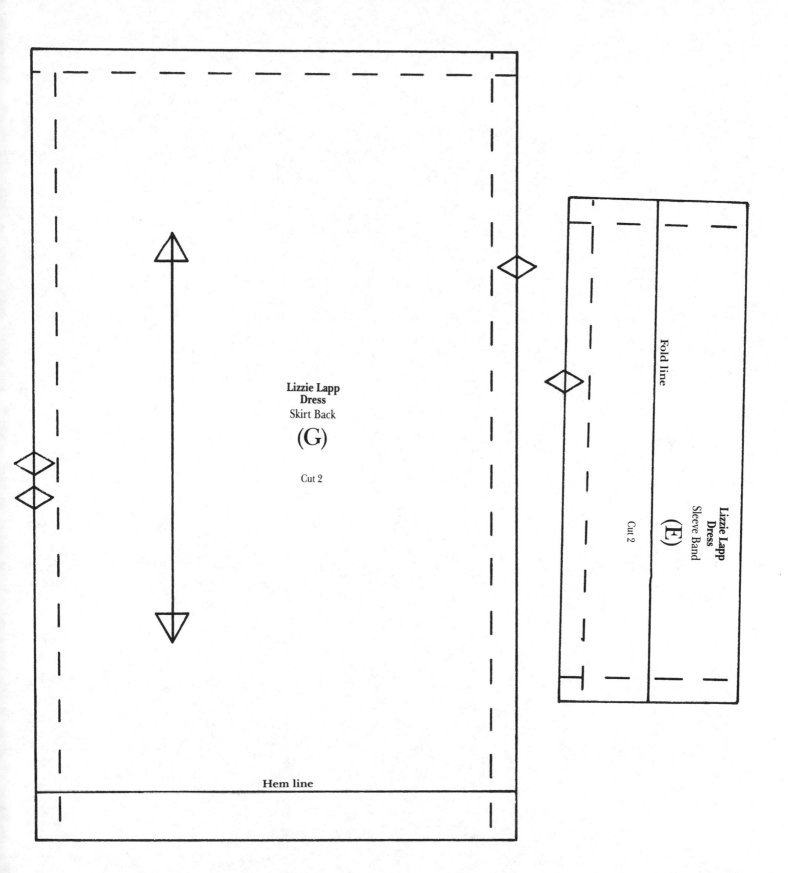

**Lizzie Lapp
Dress**
Skirt Back

(G)

Cut 2

Hem line

Fold line

**Lizzie Lapp
Dress**
Sleeve Band

(E)

Cut 2

About the Amish

A Christian religious group, the Amish trace their beginnings to the Protestant Reformation of the 16th century. Their roots extend to the Anabaptist part of that movement, which practiced adult, voluntary baptism. These reformers viewed the Bible as a normative guide for all of life, believed in separation of church and state, and refused to take part in war or any other form of violence.

One of the prominent Anabaptist leaders was Menno Simons, whose followers became known as Mennonites. The Amish are named for Jacob Amman, who split with the Mennonites in 1693 over issues concerning the maintenance of church purity.

Severely persecuted in European cities where the Anabaptist movement began, Amish and Mennonites fled to the countryside. Members of both groups came to North America in large numbers in the 1700s for the promise of religious freedom and rich farmland.

Readings and Sources

About Amish Quilts and Crafts

Bishop, Robert and Elizabeth Safanda. **A Gallery of Amish Quilts.** New York: E. P. Dutton and Co., 1976.

Haders, Phyllis. **Sunshine and Shadow: The Amish and Their Quilts.** New York: Universe Books, 1976.

Horton, Roberta. **Amish Adventure.** Lafayette, California: C & T Publishing, 1983.

Lawson, Suzy. **Amish Inspiration.** Cottage Grove, Oregon: Amity Publications, 1982.

Pellman, Rachel T. **Amish Quilt Patterns.** Intercourse, Pennsylvania: Good Books, 1984.

_____ and Kenneth Pellman. **Amish Crib Quilts.** Intercourse, Pennsylvania: Good Books, 1985.

_____ and Kenneth Pellman. **Amish Doll Quilts, Dolls, and Other Playthings.** Intercourse, Pennsylvania: Good Books, 1986.

_____ . **Small Amish Quilt Patterns.** Intercourse, Pennsylvania: Good Books, 1985.

_____ and Kenneth Pellman. **The World of Amish Quilts.** Intercourse, Pennsylvania: Good Books, 1984.

_____ and Joanne Ranck. **Quilts Among the Plain People.** Intercourse, Pennsylvania: Good Books, 1981.

Pottinger, David. **Quilts from the Indiana Amish.** New York: E. P. Dutton, Inc., 1983.

About the Amish

Amish Cooking. Aylmer, Ontario: Pathway Publishing House, 1965.

Bender, H.S. **The Anabaptist Vision.** Scottdale, Pennsylvania: Herald Press, 1967.

The Budget. Sugarcreek, Ohio, 1890– . A weekly newspaper serving the Amish and conservative Mennonite communities in North America.

Devoted Christian's Prayer Book. Aylmer, Ontario: Pathway Publishing House, 1967.

Family Life. Amish periodical publishing monthly. Aylmer, Ontario: Pathway Publishing House.

Fisher, Sara and Rachel Stahl. **The Amish School.** Intercourse, Pennsylvania: Good Books, 1985.

Gingerich, Orland. **The Amish of Canada.** Waterloo, Ontario: Conrad Press, 1972.

Good, Merle. **Who Are the Amish?** Intercourse, Pennsylvania: Good Books, 1985.

_____ and Phyllis Pellman Good. **20 Most Asked Questions about the Amish and Mennonites.** Intercourse, Pennsylvania: Good Books, 1979.

Good, Phyllis Pellman and Rachel Thomas Pellman. **From Amish and Mennonite Kitchens.** Intercourse, Pennsylvania: Good Books, 1984.

Hostetler, John A. **Amish Life.** Scottdale, Pennsylvania: Herald Press, 1959.

_____ . **Amish Society.** Baltimore: Johns Hopkins University Press, 1963.

_____ and Gertrude E. Huntingdon. **Children in Amish Society.** New York: Holt, Rinehart and Winston, 1971.

Kaiser, Grace H. **Dr. Frau: A Woman Doctor Among the Amish.** Intercourse, Pennsylvania: Good Books, 1986.

Keim, Albert N. **Compulsory Education and the Amish.** Boston: Beacon Press, 1975.

Klaasen, Walter. **Anabaptism: Neither Catholic Nor Protestant.** Waterloo, Ontario: Conrad Press, 1972.

Ruth, John L. **A Quiet and Peaceable Life.** Intercourse,

Pennsylvania: Good Books, 1985.

Scott, Stephen. **Plain Buggies.** Intercourse, Pennsylvania: Good Books, 1981.

_____ . **Why Do They Dress That Way?** Intercourse, Pennsylvania: Good Books, 1986.

_____ . **The Amish Wedding and Other Celebrations of the Old Order Communities.** Intercourse, Pennsylvania: Good Books, 1987.

Seitz, Ruth Hoover. **Amish Country.** New York: Crescent Books, 1987.

Steffy, Jan and Denny Bond, illus. **The School Picnic.** Children's book about the Amish for ages 4–8. Intercourse, Pennsylvania: Good Books, 1987.

Van Braght, Thieleman J., comp. **The Bloody Theatre;** or, **Martyrs Mirror.** Scottdale, Pennsylvania: Herald Press, 1951.

Index

About the Authors

Rachel Pellman is manager of the Old Country Store in Intercourse, Pennsylvania, which features quilts, toys and crafts made by more than 300 Amish and Mennonite artisans. She and her husband, Kenneth, are authors of *The World of Amish Quilts* and *Amish Doll Quilts, Dolls, and Other Playthings.* She also has written *Amish Quilt Patterns* and *Small Amish Quilt Patterns,* and has collaborated on *Quilts Among the Plain People, From Amish and Mennonite Kitchens* and 12 Pennsylvania Dutch cookbooks.

The Pellmans live in Lancaster, Pennsylvania, with their sons, Nathaniel and Jesse.

Jan Steffy, Leola, Pennsylvania, is a former assistant manager of The People's Place, a museum and heritage center in Intercourse. She is the author of *The School Picnic,* a children's book about the Amish.

Jan currently attends Eastern Mennonite College, Harrisonburg, Virginia.